The Unified Theory
of Profitability

D0890511

The Unified Theory of Profitability

25 Ways to Accelerate Growth Through Operational Excellence

Andrew Miller

BUSINESS EXPERT PRESS

The Unified Theory of Profitability: 25 Ways to Accelerate Growth Through Operational Excellence
Copyright © Business Expert Press, LLC, 2016

First published in 2016 by
Business Expert Press, LLC
222 East 46th Street, New York, NY 10017
www.businessexpertpress.com

ISBN-13: 978-1-63157-435-1 (paperback)
ISBN-13: 978-1-63157-436-8 (e-book)

Business Expert Press Supply and Operations Management Collection

Collection ISSN: 2156-8189 (print)
Collection ISSN: 2156-8200 (electronic)

Cover and interior design by S4Carlisle Publishing Services
Private Ltd., Chennai, India

First edition: 2016

10 9 8 7 6 5 4 3 2 1

Printed in the United States of America.

Abstract

When we discuss accelerating top line growth and maximizing profitability, we often consider hiring more people or cutting expenses or raising prices. We don't always look at ways to better exploit what we already have. Instead of hiring new people, we need to improve the performance of our current employees. Instead of cutting costs, we need better invest the money we do spend. Instead of raising prices we need to identify our ideal customers and sell to them. This book will discuss strategies on how to do all of these things and more. It will give you 25 ways to accelerate revenue growth and increase profitability immediately, without making any new financial investments. That is the Unified Theory of Profitability. It means you look at your organization and find ways to better leverage what you already have. It means focusing on those strategies that can provide the best results. It means becoming an expert on executing on those strategies.

You can do this. You just need to find the ideas that work for you and commit to implementing them.

Keywords

accelerating growth, accelerating revenue growth, boost performance, excellence, maximizing profitability, operational elegance, operational excellence, operations excellence, performance, profit margins, profitability, revenue growth, top line growth

Contents

Acknowledgments

This book would not have happened without the total support of my wife Eryn, and my three amazing children, James, Nicole, and Ellie, who are so proud that not only does their daddy write books, but also that people actually buy and read them.

To Dr. Alan Weiss, thank you for all of your advice and guidance and introducing me to Business Expert Press. I would never have one, let alone two commercially published books, without you pushing me to get my ideas out there.

To Amanda Setili, thank you for the title of this book. You once told me that my ideas were great, but they needed some unified way to express them. That was the genesis of the Unified Theory of Profitability. Once I had that title, writing this book became much easier.

To Business Expert Press, and especially Scott Isenberg, thank you for realizing the potential in my ideas and the support you provided throughout the writing of this book.

Introduction

The concepts of accelerating growth, maximizing profitability, and boosting operational performance are not new. However, we often think about increasing profits through sales or cutting expenses or raising prices. We need to improve our sales team effectiveness and sales processes. We need to improve our closing rate. We need to see more potential customers. We need to improve our pipeline. Of course, those things are all true, but they are not the only way to accelerate revenue growth and boost profits and performance.

This book will help you identify all of the ways you can maximize financial performance and increase profit, that have nothing to do with cutting costs, hiring new sales people, or raising prices. I call this the Unified Theory of Profitability.

Do you want to turn compliance into revenue? What if your procurement and supply chain employees were able to generate significant value through partnerships?

Do you want to find money where you do not normally look? Well, what if your service and repair people were able to close new business with customers?

Do you want to transform cost centers into profit centers? What if your customer service representatives were trained to sell more products and services to customers after an issue was resolved?

Do you want to convert sunk costs into assets? What if you could reduce absenteeism without spending a dime?

This book will discuss strategies on how to do all of these things and many more.

This book will give you 25 ways that you can accelerate revenue growth and increase your profits immediately, without making any new financial investments. It will show you what's possible and what you need to do to achieve your True Profit™ (the gap between your current profitability and where it could be). The only way to close that gap is to master the different profit margin levers an organization can pull. Many of those levers have nothing to do with sales. They come from operations.

Finding your True Profit™ means more effectively leveraging the assets you already have. It means applying new ideas better and maximizing the impact of those ideas.

Strap yourself in for this journey. It was be quick and painless, and very lucrative!!!

The Foundations
of Profitability

CHAPTER 1

Why True Profit™ Is Like Unmined Gold

The relentless pursuit of increased profit is every executive's dream and nightmare. The motivators can change—shareholders, the stock markets, ownership, or even an executive's compensation plan. Whatever the reason, for-profit companies are always looking for new and creative ways to increase profit. To put it simply, there are only three ways to do that:

- Increasing revenue while maintaining costs.
- Maintaining revenue while decreasing costs.
- Increasing revenue and decreasing costs.

However, within those three ways, there are many different strategies that can be employed. This book will discuss the most effective of those strategies. However, here is a hint: the organizations that will have the most success are the ones that can best take advantage of opportunities. It is not about luck and good timing. It is about finding opportunities where you do not normally look—opportunities that will have an impact, and then maximizing that impact.

The first step is determining where the opportunities are and how much of an impact can be had. That means finding your True Profit and then realizing it.

What Is True Profit?

True Profit is a new way of thinking about your opportunities to increase profit. It is a concept that I developed to help my clients maximize profitability by finding opportunities that require little to no financial investment. All you need is some discipline, some creativity, and the drive to make improvements. Understanding your organization's True Profit shows you how much money you are leaving on the table.

At one time or another, we have all said to ourselves, "I know there are opportunities to increase profitability and perform better; I just need to find and capitalize on those opportunities." That is what finding your True Profit is. The key is not only identifying those opportunities, but also capitalizing on them.

True Profit is the difference between your organization's current profit and what its potential profit could be. That potential profit is what I call True Profit. It is that profit you could be making if you were able to capitalize on opportunities. The way to realize your True Profit is by becoming a margin master—mastering the different profit margin levers and knowing when to pull which lever.

Where Is My Headlamp?

Have you ever thought to yourself, "I know there is a better way of doing this, but I am not sure where to start?" If you have, then you are like almost every other executive who wants to improve the bottom line of his or her business and organization. The challenge is finding the starting point, but more importantly, having the will to look in the deep, dark corners of your organization to find those opportunities.

We need our miner's hat and headlamp to scour those deep, dark corners and shine a light on all of the opportunities in front of us. When was the last time you reviewed your customer complaints process, or the way you manage vendor contracts, or the way you handle product returns? There is nothing sexy about any of these operations, but I guarantee that you are leaving money on the table by not looking at them. Same as the way gold prospectors often needed to explore new and strange places, you need to explore the strange places in your organization.

Here are some areas of an organization that should have the light shined on them. Not because they often perform poorly, but because most organizations just look at them as a necessary department or function. They consider them repetitive activities or compliance functions that do not add much value to the organization's bottom line.

Note: It should be noted that I use the word "compliance" very broadly in this book. I use it less to describe those departments in an organization that help it comply with government and other external regulations, and more to describe those departments that are tasked with policing the internal processes and policies that an organization has.

- Your procurement department
- Your claims department
- Your finance department
- The integration between your marketing and sales departments
- The collaboration between your sales and manufacturing areas
- Your HR department
- Your IT department
- Your supply chain
- Your customer-facing systems (online booking, website, and so on)
- Your customer service department
- Your call center

Later in the book, I will talk about why these areas, and others, are very important when trying to find your True Profit. However, here is a hint: because most organizations do not look there. They let these departments run themselves or consider them compliance areas that must adhere to strict rules and protocols. The organization looks down on them because they always seem to be getting in the way of accelerating the way the organization operates. They do not think of them as revenue-generating areas or being able to have a significant impact on the bottom line.

In consulting, we have coined the phrase "low-hanging fruit" to mean making changes and improvements that are easy and obvious. These changes can be made without much effort and can have a dramatic impact on the organization. However, once we have picked all of the low-hanging fruits, how do we reach the fruit that is higher up? The fruit that is harder to get to but will likely provide greater benefits. We need to come up with new ways to harvest that fruit.

Determining Your True Profit

As mentioned earlier, True Profit is the difference between your current profit and the profit you could be making if you were able to master the various profit margin levers (Figure 1.1).

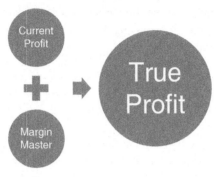

Figure 1.1 True profit

So how can you determine your True Profit? Take this assessment to help you identify the key areas of opportunity.

The True Profit Assessment

Give each statement a score from 1 to 4 (based on the scoring legend), and then total them up for each profit lever (there are nine).

	Statement	Scoring 4 = Strongly agree 3 = Moderately agree 2 = Moderately disagree 1 = Strongly disagree
1	**Pricing and Payment Terms**	
	We know when to increase and decrease our prices and measure the impact of any price change.	
	We try different pricing strategies with different customer segments.	
	We offer different payment terms to accelerate revenue collection.	
	Total score	
2	**Procurement and Managing Suppliers**	
	We distinguish between strategic and commoditized purchases and use different buying strategies for each.	

	Statement	Scoring 4 = Strongly agree 3 = Moderately agree 2 = Moderately disagree 1 = Strongly disagree
	We know who our key suppliers are and proactively manage those relationships and contracts.	
	We are able to maximize return on investment and leverage the purchases that we make.	
	Total score	
3	**Cost of Goods Sold**	
	We constantly look for ways to reduce the cost of goods sold without impacting the quality of the product.	
	We minimize defects, wasted materials, and failure work.	
	We are able to control our costs.	
	Total score	
4	**Supply Chain Optimization**	
	We constantly review the supply chain to minimize the number of touch points.	
	We optimize inventory and distribution strategies (increase inventory turnover, reduce lead times).	
	We share information with customers and suppliers to maintain control of supply and demand.	
	Total score	
5	**Customer Growth and Retention**	
	We know who our target customers are and the value that we can offer them.	
	We help our existing customers become ambassadors for our organization.	
	We stratify our customers and treat each customer segment differently.	
	Total score	

(Continued)

	Statement	Scoring 4 = Strongly agree 3 = Moderately agree 2 = Moderately disagree 1 = Strongly disagree
6	**Employee Empowerment and Retention**	
	We empower employees to practice excellence on the front lines by allowing them the freedom to make decisions and fail.	
	We identify and cultivate our top potential employees and give them additional responsibility and recognition.	
	We are an organization that people line up to join.	
	Total score	
7	**Brand Recognition**	
	New customers seek us out.	
	We are well known by our customers and prospective customers.	
	We are actively involved in helping advance our industry and our community.	
	Total score	
8	**Operational Excellence**	
	We align our daily tactics with the overall strategy of the organization and can measure how those tactics help us execute the strategy.	
	We encourage employees to challenge the status quo and use common sense and good judgment.	
	We look for money and performance boosts in areas that other organizations do not normally look at.	
	Total score	
9	**Innovating and Collaborating**	
	We measure the adoption rate of new ideas and the impact they have on overall company performance (i.e., a Vitality index).	
	We foster an environment that encourages employees, suppliers, customers, and business partners to bring new ideas forward.	
	We encourage collaboration, both internal and external, to broaden the impact of ideas.	
	Total score	

True Profit vs. Actual Profit

To calculate your True Profit, enter the score from the assessment for each lever. Add 0.5 percent for every lever where you scored less than nine, and 1 percent for every score less than six. Totaling these up provides your True Profit.

	Assessment Score	True Profit
Pricing and payment terms		
Procurement and managing suppliers		
Cost of goods sold		
Supply chain optimization		
Customer growth and retention		
Employee empowerment and retention		
Brand recognition		
Operational excellence		
Innovating and collaborating		
Your Total True Profit		

Your true profit is the minimum amount of additional profit you can achieve by implementing the right strategies in the right areas.

When I recently used this assessment with a client, they realized that, conservatively speaking, they could increase profit margins by at least 5 percent by changing some processes and implementing some new performance metrics. No new large investments were required. Just a better focus on making the changes in areas that they know will lead to more profit.

This organization, like many, knew that they had opportunities to improve financial performance. In addition, like many organizations, they struggled with identifying where the best opportunities were and how to take the first step. Once organizations take the first step, it is easier to take subsequent steps. In this case, the first step was taking the group performing some of the processes and activities that had been identified, and asking them for suggestions on what improvements could be made. My client was shocked at the number of great ideas that surfaced.

We then had to figure out which of the ideas to implement. We created a committee to review the ideas based on some common criteria that we developed (potential impact on the bottom line, ease of implementation, sustainability, and others), so that the best ideas bubbled to the surface. My client then put together a plan to maximize the results from those ideas, including who was accountable for the success or failure of the execution of the ideas, and how success would be measured.

Almost immediately, they were able to start making changes and saw a dramatic improvement within the first 6 months, with profit increasing by almost 5 percent in that time. We continued to roll this out across the organization and made additional changes that aligned with the direction my client wanted to go. The keys to success were spending the time to determine the best ideas and having the discipline to only implement a few ideas at a time.

Ryanair Rises Above the Clouds to Find Its True Profit

Ryanair is Europe's biggest low-cost airline. It has always been criticized for its poor service and laissez-faire attitude toward customers who wanted anything more than a low-priced airfare. Michael O'Leary, who runs the airline, has even been known to criticize passengers for being "idiots." But in late 2013, Ryanair refocused its business to attract new customers and retain more of its existing customers. Ryanair's old model of service was to be the lowest cost provider, not lose customers' baggage, and to have flights arrive on time. Everything else was ignored. Not exactly the textbook strategy for customer acquisition and retention.

By the end of 2013, Ryanair began to change its definition of customer service and change its culture toward one of customer focus. It eliminated many of the policies that were frustrating customers and allowed more carry-on baggage, reduced penalties, and allowed customers to book an assigned seat. One of the more visible ways it made changes was to overhaul the online booking system. It reduced the number of steps customers had to take from 17 to 5. Imagine the difference that would make if you were a customer. Imagine having to go through 17 different steps to book a simple flight.

Profits jumped by 32 percent in the first 6 months after these changes were made. Customer complaints went down by 40 percent, and the airline anticipates an annual profit that will be 45 percent higher from the previous year. They attracted 4 percent more passengers over the summer period. Those are some significant results.

So what will Ryanair do with all of this newfound profit? Invest it back in the business by buying 200 new planes with the goal of doubling the size of the company. Not bad for a company that only a year before had very little focus on customer service outside of being the lowest cost provider.

The following can be learned from what Ryanair has accomplished:

- Strategy is fluid and organizations need to be flexible and nimble enough to change quickly.
- There can be significant profit increases without making large capital investments. Many of the changes Ryanair made were to internal policies and procedures, and the behaviors of their people.
- Making additional profit allows an organization to reinvest in the business.
- Being the lowest cost provider of anything can only go so far. At some point, it becomes saturated and an organization needs to offer more to attract and retain customers.
- The most successful organizations have leaders who exhibit the behaviors they want others to exhibit. Michael O'Leary of Ryanair had to change his own approach to customer service before he could ask his employees to do so.
- Organizations need clarity in the direction they want to go and the tactics they employ must align with this. Eliminating policies and processes that were frustrating to customers went a long way in helping Ryanair change customer perception of the organization.

Home Depot Exhibits Do-It-Yourself Profit Improvement

The success of do-it-yourself home improvement giant Home Depot has always been tied to the housing market. When the housing market is booming and people are buying more houses, they want to upgrade their fixtures and invest more money in the new house. When the market is slow, fewer homes are being turned over, people invest less in new homes, and do-it-yourself projects tend to be smaller.

From 2011 to 2014, Home Depot's profit margin increased from 6.74 percent to 8.61 percent (source: http://ycharts.com/companies/HD/profit_margin). That is more than a 25 percent increase in profit margins over 3 years. The financial analysts will tell you that it is because the housing market was hot, which led to higher customer traffic through Home Depot stores and an increase in same store sales. These things are true, but they do not tell the whole story and do not necessarily mean more profitability. During that same time period, Home Depot also took a huge reputational hit when data for thousands of customers were breached. Yet, still profits rose.

If it was not just the hot housing market, what did Home Depot do that allowed it to have such tremendous success?

- It adapted marketing efforts to suit the housing market. When the market was booming, it marketed bigger home improvement projects and when it slowed down, Home Depot marketed smaller projects.
- It slowed down global growth and expansion and focused more on maximizing results from the stores and people it already had invested in.
- Like Ryanair, it put more focus on the customer experience by updating stores to be more open and appealing, and encouraging staff to roam the stores looking for customers who needed help.
- It expanded into different product areas trying to increase brand awareness. You can now see the Home Depot logo on toys in children's toys stores.
- It began offering free in-store workshops and seminars, teaching customers and prospective customers the best ways to complete certain do-it-yourself projects.

Essentially, Home Depot did a better job of leveraging the assets it already had and maximizing results from those assets, which were its people, its brand, and its locations. This led to an increase in the average sale size per customer and a better customer experience.

What We Learned?

True Profit is a concept that any organization can achieve. The following are the keys to success for your organization in order to realize its True Profit:

- Look for opportunities in areas you would not normally look.
- Figure out how to transform cost centers into profit centers.
- Turn compliance into revenue.
- Use common criteria to assess and compare different opportunities.
- Have the discipline to only select a small number of opportunities for implementation.
- Ensure one person is accountable for the success or failure of the implementation.
- Plan the activities and the metrics to be used to determine success and ensure they align with the direction the organization wants to go.
- Engage the people most impacted by the change early and often.
- Look for areas of your operation that can be improved, and take the first step.
- Convert sunk costs into assets.

These create the foundation for *the Unified Theory of Profitability* that will be introduced in Chapter 3.

Finding your organization's True Profit does not always mean cutting costs or increasing revenues. It can often mean getting more out of what you have already invested in. It can mean finding opportunities in areas that you would not normally consider. It can mean removing obstacles that hinder profitability.

CHAPTER 2

Developing a Low Center of Gravity

I grew up playing hockey as a defenseman. I was never the fastest skater or the most skilled. The one thing I was very good at was cutting down the angles when opposing players would come down, and try and score. Once I started playing contact hockey, I discovered something even more important—having a low center of gravity allowed me to knock down even the tallest player.

It did not matter how big or tall the player was. By combining speed with my power and coming it at the right angle, I was able to knock anybody over. As you can imagine, this came in very handy. I recently began thinking about how this applies to organizations. You do not have to be the biggest or the strongest organization in order to knock over the obstacles in your way. You just need to understand the importance of speed, angle, and impact in order to exploit your low center of gravity as an organization.

Organizations that have a low center of gravity can absorb hits taken from the competition and bounce back or even knock the competition over. These organizations can knock over obstacles in their way. They brace themselves for changes in the market or competition, and are ready to strike when the time is right.

The Importance of Speed, Power, and Angles

The reason having a low center of gravity is so important for an organization is that it allows you to maximize impact. In hockey, that means knocking the other player off the puck and taking it from them. In business, it can mean a lot of different things. Most importantly, it means that you are able to maximize the impact of whatever you are doing.

As an organization, you want to maximize impact wherever possible, and in order to do that you need to create a low center of gravity. In order to create that low center of gravity, organizations need to master three elements:

1. Speed: You need to approach any initiative or strategy with speed. That does not mean you need to put the pedal to the metal. It means you need to arrive with the optimum speed—speed that is as fast as you can go without compromising the quality of what you are doing.
2. Angle: You need to take the right approach and have the right angle. You need to come in from the right angle in order to maximize impact. That means being deliberate about how you approach an opportunity or challenge.
3. Power: You need to come with strength and power. You do not always have to come in with the maximum amount of power, but it needs to be enough to have the impact you are looking for.

If any of these three elements are missing, you will not be able to maximize impact and go through the obstacles in your way. Figure 2.1 shows the sweet spot between the three elements and what happens if you are not in that sweet spot.

If you have speed and power (area #1), but come in from the wrong angle, you will miss your target.

When an airplane makes its approach for a landing, it must come from the appropriate angle in order to land smoothly and on the runway.

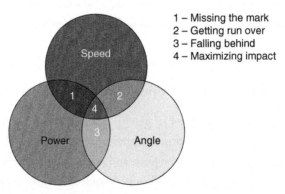

Figure 2.1 Finding your center of gravity

Even if it comes in with the right speed and power, if it comes in from the wrong angle, it will miss the runway and/or hit the ground too firmly. Many of us have had situations where planes have circled the airport to ensure the right approach angle. Without it, the risk of disaster increases dramatically.

If you have speed and come in from the right angle (area #2) but do not have enough power, you will get run over.

If you have ever watched a video of a spaceship trying to land, you will know what I mean. Even at the right speed and with the right angle, without the thrusters (the power) to balance it, the spaceship would tip over or miss its mark. Organizations need those same thrusters to ensure everything stays level.

If you come in from the right angle and have enough power (area #3) but not enough speed, you will be left behind. Your competitors will fly right by you.

When newspapers first went digital, they assumed that all of their readers would come with them. Therefore, they put all of their articles and content behind paid subscription services. If you wanted to read the article, you needed to pay a monthly fee. As we now know, those paid subscription services did not work. It was not about their approach or power as much as it was about their speed. They were too late to the party. By the time most of these newspapers moved their content online, there were already a plethora of digital sites where readers could get the news for free. The paid services the newspapers were offering did not offer any additional value to justify the fee; so most customers (except for those extremely loyal to their preferred newspaper) found other outlets for getting their news.

If you have the right speed, the right amount of power, and you come in from the right angle, you will maximize impact.

The following are some ways to ensure you develop the right center of gravity:

- Know what your optimal speed is. How fast can your organization go and still be effective?
- Know what obstacles you are trying to overcome. What are the opportunities where you want to maximize impact?

- Know what your organization's strengths are. Where can you bring the full power of your organization to bear?
- Know which opportunity presents the greatest impact and how you will exploit it. What is the most effective way to exploit that opportunity?

Let us review a couple of these in more detail.

Finding Your Organization's Optimal Speed

Although it may sound counterintuitive, speed is not always about going faster. Sometimes you need to slow down to get the best results. But how do you know when to slow down and when to speed up?

Think of your organization as a train system. The signals on the track are the indicators telling you when to slow down and when to speed up depending on a whole bunch of factors. The stations are the different milestones along the way, getting you to your ultimate destination. The speed of other trains, passenger emergencies, the weather, track maintenance, volume, and many other things can impact the speed of the train. If the train slows down at the wrong time, it will fall behind schedule. If it goes too fast, it might risk a crash because the tracks can only handle a certain speed, or it might catch up to the train in front of it. The train needs to go at optimal speed to meet its schedule.

You need to create your own schedule based on how fast you can go in order to achieve the best results. Then you need to put indicators in place to track the progress that needs to be made—similar to the train system.

These signals are the measurements and indicators you use to show progress and monitor performance. These are your indicators for achieving optimal speed. Look at the different areas of your business—product commercialization, strategy development, customer acquisition, employee hiring, and any others that are important for your organization—and ask yourself if you have achieved optimal speed. How would you know? What process would you go through to determine the optimal speed?

I take some of my clients through a process to determine the optimal speed for their organizations. Here are the questions we begin with for each of their key areas:

- How fast are you currently going?
- How fast could you go (what is your optimal speed)?
- What impact would it have if you achieved optimal speed (positively or negatively)?
- What are the key indicators we should use to determine when to slow down and when to speed up?
- What plan do we need to put in place to maintain optimal speed?

We often use the wrong indicators to measure performance, because we focus on pure speed and going faster, not governing speed.

> We measure customer service representatives on how fast they complete phone calls, not whether or not the customer's issue was resolved on the first call.
>
> We measure speed of product to market without considering the quality of that product or whether or not it was a commercial success.
>
> We measure the time it takes to hire new employees even though we have had high employee turnover rates in the past.
>
> We measure the time it takes to process a purchase order but not if the purchase order was correct.

These are all examples of focusing on moving faster, but we can all agree that these outcomes would be detrimental to an organization's results. There are times when going too fast will hurt the organization, just as there are times when going too slow will impact its performance. The most successful organizations are able to move at their optimal speed at all times, and they recognize that optimal speed will change depending on the situation.

They are also able to apply that optimal speed when creating their low center of gravity to knock over the obstacles in their way.

Finding the Right Obstacles to Knock Over

When I first realized that I could knock over bigger opponents in hockey, I became a pinball, trying to knock over anyone and everyone. However, that was not always what was best for my team. Understanding when to knock over the right player, in the right situation, was much more powerful. Doing that provides more impact when it does happen, and it reduces the risk of failure (which in a hockey sense would mean turning the puck over to the other team).

You need to have some guidelines to identify the right obstacles to knock over. Those obstacles could be internal ones (bureaucracy or departmental silos) or external (regulatory issues or new competition). Here are some questions to help you identify the most important obstacles to knock over:

- If we remove or knock over the obstacle, will it clear a path for us to exploit an opportunity that we would not have been otherwise able to exploit?
- If we remove or knock over the obstacle, what will be the benefit?
- Are we able to knock over the obstacle without the help of others (outside of the organization)?
- Will we need to do something we are not comfortable with in order to knock over the obstacle?

You need to ensure that you are knocking over the right obstacles and using your low center of gravity to its maximum impact. I always prided myself in delivering clean body checks—the opposing players' back was never turned and they were usually expecting the check to come so that they could prepare for it.

Aim properly by directing your power, speed, and angle to the right initiatives. Otherwise, you will be knocking over obstacles just for the sake of it. In hockey, that is the difference between a goon (someone who just runs people over) and a contributor (a player who provides a physical presence but can also score). Goons have very short careers and provide very limited value. Contributors have long careers and provide value to their teams in many different ways.

Are you a goon or a contributor?

How Low Is Too Low?

One of my favorite songs by the band Little Feat is called *Texas Twister*. The words in the chorus go, "How fast is too fast, how high is too high?..."

When discussing your center of gravity, we also need to consider, how low is too low?

If your center of gravity is too low, then the competition will leap right over you. If it is too high, then you will be undercut. You need to determine where your center of gravity is the strongest, which takes us back to the beginning of the chapter when I discussed speed, angle, and power. Speed gives you enough momentum to run things over; angle gives you the right direction for approach; and power gives you the thrust to stay level as you run things over.

Let us try a real-life example of what I mean. I was working with a client who wanted to rapidly increase sales growth. In order to do that, I helped them identify those forces that were for and against the achievement of that objective. We looked at what forces would help them achieve rapid, dramatic sales growth, and what factors would hinder it. Figure 2.2 shows these forces.

By charting out these forces, we were able to determine the right center of gravity for the organization. In order to achieve the right speed, approach from the right angle, and to have enough power, we needed to exploit those forces aiding in rapid sales growth and eliminate those forces against it. Here are some of the strategies we implemented to

Figure 2.2 Forces influencing dramatic and rapid sales growth

ensure my client had a low enough center of gravity to grow sales quickly and sustainably:

- Developed a clear vision of who were my client's ideal prospective customers.
- Tailored the message to those ideal prospective customers so that it was easy to deliver by all employees and spoke to the needs of the ideal customer base.
- Leverage my client's existing customers to identify new prospective customers who met the vision of an ideal customer.
- Gave employees more accountability for finding and onboarding these ideal customers.

My client grew sales by almost 10 percent in the first year they implemented these strategies. They were also able to maintain that low center of gravity and sustain sales growth for another 2 years.

CHAPTER 3

Creating Your Hydraulic Profit Jack

I was speaking with a colleague a few months ago, telling her about the concept for this book. I mentioned that I had identified all these different ways to accelerate growth and increase profitability without making any new capital investment. She asked me about some of them, I told her some of my best ideas, and she replied, "You need some common or unified way of describing all of these different strategies because they are in so many different areas." And that is how the Unified Theory of Profitability was born.

We need to change the way we think about accelerating growth and increasing profitability in our organizations. Many organizations still default to old ways of thinking—raising prices, continuously cutting costs, or adding new sales people as the only ways to increase revenues and profitability. But that leaves so much opportunity on the table.

We need to be able to better leverage the assets we already have, and turn compliance departments into revenue generators—cost centers into profit centers. We need to be able to find opportunities where we do not normally look. Figure 3.1 lays it out for us.

The Unified Theory of Profitability means we are able to turn sunk costs into assets. We can turn compliance into revenue (remember from Chapter 1 that compliance refers more to adherence with internal policies and procedures). We can find money where we do not normally look. And we can transform cost centers into profit centers.

The following are some specific examples of what I mean:

- Can you train your customer service representatives to offer customers new products and services once they have resolved a customer's issue?

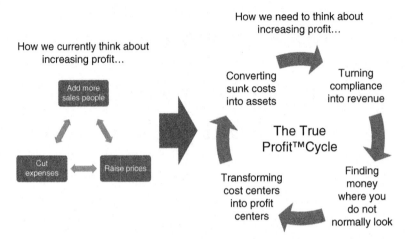

Figure 3.1 The unified theory of profitability

- Have you developed something for internal use that can be commercialized (an IT system or a tool)?
- Can you build stronger partnerships to increase value from your relationships with suppliers?
- Can you develop your account managers to focus on growth with their assigned customers instead of merely managing the account?

These are just a few examples of how to increase profitability without cutting costs or making any new capital investments.

Why Cost Centers Make No Sense

Currently, can any company afford to have a department or division that does not contribute to the top or bottom line? The concept of a cost center makes no sense. "Let's develop a department where we incur costs and have no ties whatsoever to improve the overall financial performance of the organization. We will have no financial measures that help the overall company improve."

So, here is where you say, "But not all departments can be tied directly to the financial performance of the overall organization!" Want to bet?

IT departments may have developed some great new technology tools to manage information in the company. Could not that be commercialized and sold?

Call center representatives, who talk to customers all day long, can be trained on all of your company's offerings and help identify new customer needs that can be filled with those products and services.

Repair people and technicians can be trained to provide better solutions to customers while they are in the field. Procurement departments can negotiate better relationships with key suppliers. Finance departments can find more cost-effective ways to report on financial information.

In addition, any department can contribute new ideas to help with customer acquisition and retention, or revenue growth, or increasing profitability.

I think you get the point. Creating cost centers is an outdated idea that needs to become extinct. Are you one of the people giving it CPR to try to keep it alive?

The Unified Theory of Profitability encourages us to think of ways to raise revenues and profits by using less effort. Think of a jack for your car. Many of us have manual tire jacks in the trunk to be used in an emergency. Those jacks are slow and take a great deal of effort and time. Usually, we cannot afford that time and effort. So imagine a hydraulic jack, like the ones used in a repair shop. It is quick and easy to use, and requires minimal effort. That is what you need to create—a hydraulic jack for profit and growth. A way for you to grow profits and revenues quickly and with little effort. I am here to show you how to build a hydraulic profit jack.

25 Ways to Increase Profit and Accelerate Growth

The next 25 chapters lay out 25 different ways you can accelerate growth and increase profits in your organization without making any new capital investments. Those 25 strategies are broken up in to eight separate categories:

1. **E Equals MC Squared** (Chapters 4–7): Emotion equals customer continuance. The focus for this category is customers and how building an emotional connection will improve retention and growth with those customers. These four chapters provide you with strategies on how to grow using your current customer base, transitioning

customers to higher margin products, and implementing new strategies to attract and retain your ideal customer better.

2. **Maximizing Power at the Point of Attack** (Chapters 8–11): These four chapters focus on employee engagement and empowerment on the frontlines. Your frontline employees are the ones who interact with customers all day long; so you need to ensure they are passionate about the organization and empowered to make decisions. These chapters focus on empowering frontline people, implementing strategy successfully across the organization, and setting expectations and measuring performance to maximize success.

3. **Doing the High Jump, Not the Limbo** (Chapters 12–15): These four chapters focus on your ideas of not only how to increase the quality of your ideas, but also how to become more innovative and opportunistic, identifying your best ideas, and maximizing the impact of those ideas. Innovation is not just about being creative and disruptive; it is also about capitalizing on and exploiting your best ideas.

4. **Taking Procurement out of the Basement** (Chapters 16 and 17): These chapters show how you can turn a compliance function into a revenue-generating one. Procurement is often considered a compliance function meant to use procedures to help organizations buy goods and services. These two chapters focus on how to leverage your procurement function to become better advisers to the organization to better leverage the assets you have already paid for, increase return on investment on purchasing dollars, and better manage relationships with suppliers and partners to increase profitability.

5. **The TAO of Cost Minimization** (Chapter 18): The focus of this chapter is looking at three key ways that your organization loses money and performance (Theft, Absenteeism, and Obsolescence) and identifies ways to minimize them in order to improve your bottom line.

6. **Supply Chain Optimization** (Chapters 19–22): These chapters focus on the supply chain—the manufacturing, movement, and storage of goods. The focus of these chapters is leveraging your supply chain to accelerate growth and increase profitability. In these chapters, I identify ways to profit from returns, defects and waste, leverage your supply chain to generate profits, reduce the number

of touch points in your supply chain, and lower inventory by better anticipating customer demand.

7. **Operational Excellence** (Chapters 23–27): These four chapters focus on ways to accelerate growth and maximize profitability by pursuing excellence, not perfection. I discuss ways to find opportunities in areas you do not normally look, how to not over deliver on customer expectations, leveraging technology to achieve your strategic goals faster, and how to bring new customers on more quickly and effectively.

8. **Your Market Crystal Ball** (Chapter 28): The final chapter focuses on how to better assess and exploit new opportunities. Too many organizations pursue every opportunity that comes their way and it hurts their ability to grow quickly and successful. This chapter gives you strategies on how to identify those opportunities that can have the biggest impact.

You do not need to implement all 25 of these strategies, but there are enough of them that you also need to find one or two that will work for you.

How to Pick the Best Strategies

If you go back to the self-assessment from Chapter 1, you will have some ideas as to where the best opportunities lie. If you want a simpler way to determine which of the eight categories to focus on, try these questions:

- As you were reading the eight categories, which one of them resonated most? Which one did you say, "That is exactly the issue I need resolved?"
- Which category best covers opportunities/issues you hear about frequently in your organization?
- Which category affords the greatest opportunity to accelerate growth and/or increase profitability?

Inevitably, one or two of the categories stood out more than the others. Start with those. If you like, go right to those chapters and start reading. The goal of this book is to provide you with practical strategies that you can implement right away; so go find them.

PROFITABILITY CATEGORY #1

E Equals MC Squared

Customer loyalty is one of the key factors in growing your profitability. You need to have a stable of customers who come back and buy your products and services. This creates a foundation or a springboard for you to take off from.

One of the biggest misconceptions in business is that a happy customer is a loyal customer. Many organizations (including some of my clients) score very high on customer satisfaction surveys, yet struggle to retain their customers. Who cares if customers are happy if they do not stay?

Instead of having blind acceptance that the customer is always right because they are happy, organizations need to focus on stratifying their customers. Who are your best customers (your "A" customers)? Why are they your best customers? How will you treat them differently? Who are your "B" customers and how will you treat them? Not all customers are created equal.

Once you acknowledge that customer stratification is important, and understand that there are only three aspects to customer relationships, you can then implement the right strategies and spend time with the right customers. The only three aspects to customer relationships that matter are:

1. Repeat business—gathering more business from existing customers
2. Referral business—acquiring new customers through your existing customer base
3. Lack of complaint—retaining customers by avoiding doing anything to cause them to complain

$E=MC^2$ is the resulting equation from the implementation of strategies that create customer loyalty.

E = Emotion (making an emotional connection with customers)

M = Mastering profit margin levers

C^2 = Customer continuance

Therefore, if you are able to create an emotional connection with your customers, then you will be able to maximize profit margins and ensure your customers come back.

In the next four chapters, we will explore different strategies on how to increase your customer loyalty and how to leverage that loyalty to accelerate and grow profitability.

CHAPTER 4

Creating Growth Through Your Best Customers

The fastest and easiest way to grow your business is through your existing customers. Full stop. Do not go any further. End of chapter.

Seriously, of course, it is important to acquire new customers to help with the sustainability of your organization, but if you are looking to accelerate growth and profitability, which is the theme of this book, then the first place you need to look is your existing customers.

Figure 4.1 shows the different ways that you can grow with customers.

You can sell existing products and services to existing customers (Status Quo).

You can sell new products and services to existing customers (Profitability).

You can sell existing products and services to new customers (Growth).

You can sell new products and services to new customers (Expansion).

Experience will show that if your business is in Status Quo, then you are actually declining, and the hardest way to increase profitability is through Expansion. Therefore, we are left with selling new products and services to existing customers, and selling existing products and services to new customers. Which one do you think can have an immediate impact on your organization's profitability?

If you said selling new products to existing customers, then you win the prize. Here is why:

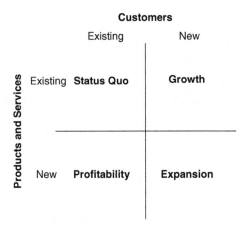

Figure 4.1 Growing your business

Your existing customers have already purchased something, and so they are familiar with what you do well.

They have already opened their bank accounts and purchased something from you. You are no longer an unknown to them. So, assuming you at least met their expectations the first time they bought something from you, there is no reason why they would not want to buy more stuff from you.

Therefore, the main reason that customers do not buy more stuff from you is because they do not know what else you offer. Do not assume they know. Assume they do not know and that you have to take every opportunity to tell them.

Costco does a very good job of selling more to its existing customers. In order to shop at Costco, you need to be a member, so that they know exactly who their customers are. They have created a loyal group of customers who shop with them regularly. Costco previously offered only bulk purchases—house supplies, food, beauty products, and so on, but soon realized that they had a captive audience and tonnes of real estate in their stores. Now they offer TVs, sporting goods, clothes, and a lot more items. They took their captive audience and offered them more.

The following are some ways you create the emotional connection with your existing customers that will lead to them buying more products and services from you:

- Offer them access to exclusive products or services (something they can only get from you).
- Treat them like VIPs and make them feel like they are your only customer.
- Offer them input into the development of your new products and services.
- Offer them information and insight not provided elsewhere.
- Onboard them quickly and easily (see Chapter 28 for more details on this).

If you want to increase profitability quickly, start with your existing customers. What else can you offer them that would be of value? What else are they buying elsewhere that they are not buying from you? How can you educate them on what else you offer? If you communicate what you have available and create that emotional connection that keeps them coming back for more, you will see your profits rise.

CHAPTER 5

Eliminating Zero-Margin and Low-Margin Products and Services

Do you know which of your products and services are profitable and which ones are not?

If you do not know, you better find out. How can you make strategic decisions if you do not know where your money is made?

As an MBA student, I worked on a group project for a distribution company. This company distributed more than 100 different newspapers across the country. We analyzed each of those newspapers independently to assess their financial contribution to the company. We found that only 36 of the more than 100 newspapers were profitable for the distribution company. Only one-third of the products they delivered were profitable. That meant everything else was losing the company money. Our advice to them: Get rid of two-thirds of your offerings and focus on growing the ones that make money.

This had not happened previously, because it was a poorly run organization or because it had a weak management team. They had just never looked at the information the way we did. They believed that because they were already delivering newspapers to certain areas of the country, it only made sense to deliver additional newspapers to those same parts of the country. A very logical business decision, right?

The problem is that business is not always about logic. It is about business. More often than not, it is about money. So, although it may make reasonable sense to add more newspapers to a truck already going to a geographic area, it may not make financial sense.

Therefore, what can you do to identify what is profitable and what is not? First, start with a list of everything that customers pay for. What are the sources of revenue for your organization? Now allocate costs to those sources of revenue. Do not make this too complicated at first. Get a ballpark figure because spending too much time and detail on this will take your focus away from what you are trying to accomplish – which is getting an initial sense of where you are making money and where you are losing money.

Where are you making money and where are you losing money? Where are profit margins either nonexistent or very small?

Now you can split your revenue sources into three groups:

- Those products and/or services with strong margins that we will keep offering and want to grow
- Those products and services with weaker margins but with an opportunity to improve those margins
- Those products and services with weak or no margins that we need to stop offering

Let us talk about the third group first—products and services you need to stop offering. At this point, you are asking, "how do I stop offering those products and services?"

Simple. You just stop. Next time someone asks you for that product, you tell them you are no longer offering it. Next time someone wants that service you have offered for 15 years, you tell them you no longer provide that service.

If you want to make the transition easier, then find a more profitable alternative to provide to the customer. "We no longer offer product X, but you might want to try product Y, which does the same thing and lasts longer." Sometimes you will not have an alternative to offer and that customer will go away. That is all right.

Not every customer is a good customer

Here are some ways to let go of your zero- and low-margin business:

- Offer an alternative produce or service that has higher margins.
- Stop offering it altogether and focus on growing your higher-margin business.

- Set up a business partnership and refer customers looking for those products and services to someone else.
- Sell that portion of the business to another company.

It does not really matter how you do it, it is just important that you do it. Companies make tough decisions all the time.

Twenty years ago, it would have been unheard of that IBM did not make computers or that Sony does not make portable music players, but it happened. Just like now, it might be unheard of that in 20 years GM will not make software for cars, only the physical cars themselves.

If we want to stay relevant, our companies need to constantly evolve. If we want to stay profitable, we have to get rid of our sacred cows. That means letting go of some things in order to reach out further.

With growth comes discomfort, and with discomfort comes progress. Are you willing to let go in order to grow?

CHAPTER 6

Transitioning Your Worst Customers to High-Margin Products and Services

In Chapter 5, we grouped your products and services into three areas:

- Those products and/or services with strong margins that we will keep offering and want to grow
- Those products and services with weaker margins but with an opportunity to improve those margins
- Those products and services with weak or no margins that we need to stop offering

We discussed what to do with the third group; now let us talk about how to capitalize on the first group—those products and services with strong margins where we want to grow. Again, we start with your existing customers and ask the question, "How can we transition our worst customers to these products and services?"

First, we need to tackle why you would even do that. Why focus on our worst customers? Because they are still customers. They still buy from you, and they still want to buy more from you. They are your worst customers, because they buy small items and make big demands. They take a great deal of effort to manage. But what if you could transition them to buying big items? They would still make big demands, but would be paying more money to have those demands met. What if you could figure out a way to offer them a product or service that met their demands more, thus reducing their need to interact with you (I call this *operational transparency*, which I cover in more detail in Chapter 26.)?

The following are some criteria for determining who your worst customers are:

- The hardest ones to acquire—you needed to pursue them constantly and persistently before they finally became a customer. They came into your store numerous times, or they called your hotline and asked lots of questions, or they required a lot of detail in the acquisition process.
- The ones who expect service levels that are not commensurate with the level of purchases they make. They buy inexpensive things but expect white-glove service.
- The ones who make small purchases and require a great deal of after-sales support. They are constantly returning items, asking for discounts, or calling saying that the product or service is not working as planned. They do not use the self-help resources you provide and want to always speak with a live person.

Take a few minutes right now and think about your customers. Who are some of the customers that come to mind based on the aforementioned criteria? Who are the customers you wish you did not have to deal with but refuse to let go of?

Write their names in the spaces below (and make sure they do not see your copy of this book).

_____

_____

_____

_____

_____

You only have two choices of what to do with these customers: You can move them to more profitable products and services, or you let them go. A third, but not viable option, is to keep them where they are and continue to eat up and frustrate your own people.

How do you determine which one to do? You need to ask yourself a few different questions:

- Why are they buying from us?
  - Do they have other options, or are you the only game in town? Are you much cheaper than the competition?
- Is there an opportunity to grow with this customer?
  - Aside from the more profitable product or service you want to move them to, are there other growth opportunities?
- Could they become an ambassador for our organization?
  - Sometimes the biggest dissenters can be turned into the biggest supporters once you determine what triggers their behavior. If you are able to find that trigger, you may be able to cultivate a completely new group of customer evangelists.

If the answer to all of these questions is "Yes" for a specific customer, then you should be investing some time in that customer by asking, "How do I most quickly and effectively take advantage of this growth opportunity?"

List five customers for which you answered "Yes" to all three questions given earlier (having none is not an option, I have no doubt there are customers that would fit into this category).

_____

_____

_____

_____

_____

Now that you have determined that there are some customers you can move to more profitable products and services, here is how to do it:

1. Meet with them to better understand their needs.
   You may have never met with them before and they may just require a little attention. Gain a better understanding of their needs and desired outcomes, and offer alternatives that will help meet those needs and desired outcomes and still meet your goals of higher profitability and less labor.
2. Tell them you no longer offer the product or service that they are currently buying.

A good friend of mine who is an executive coach stopped offering long, inexpensive coaching engagements, and replaced them with more valuable and intimate coaching programs. These new programs provided better results for the people being coached and higher revenues for her.

When contemplating what to do with your worst customers, you are ultimately answering the question, "Is there anything I can offer where I would be happy keeping this customer?" That might mean they spend more money, or contacting you less, or telling others about you. Most of these customers you will want to let go of.

However, before doing so across the board, find few of those who can represent some unmined gold for your organization.

CHAPTER 7

Implementing Customer Retention Strategies on the Frontlines

Organizations should always be focusing on customer retention, because it is the fastest way to accelerate growth. Your existing customers already know your organization and what you offer; so it is easy to offer them new products and services as well as help them become ambassadors to help you attract new customers. But how much effort are you putting into retaining customers you *do not* want? My guess is, too much.

This phenomenon is not just about not letting these customers go, which is passive. I could live with that. The issue is that you are actively trying to retain these customers. This means you are taking time and effort away from retaining the customers you *do* want.

Maximizing overall customer retention is not always good. Not all customers are good customers, and not all business is good business, as we have already established. Customer retention is only effective if you are retaining the customers you want. I call this concept *purposeful customer retention reduction*. Yes, I know that is a bit of a mouthful to say, but the concept should be easy to remember. Purposeful customer retention reduction is the act of not retaining certain customers, because they are not your ideal customers. You consciously decide not to retain them because they take time and resources away from your ideal customers. So, you let them go. Yes, that is right, you let them go (this should not be a new concept for you if you read Chapter 6).

Review Figure 7.1 and ask yourself in which quadrant your organization fits (be honest).

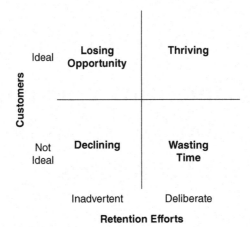

Figure 7.1 Purposeful customer retention reduction

If your retention efforts are inadvertent and helping to retain customers who are not ideal, then you are declining. You are keeping the customers you do not want and losing the ones you do want.

If your retention efforts are deliberate but targeted at the wrong customers, you are wasting time (bottom right). You are utilizing resources in the wrong places. You are putting resources into retaining customers you do not want, while the ones you do want are walking down the street right in front of you (figuratively speaking). More than two-thirds of the companies I encounter fall into this quadrant.

If your retention efforts are inadvertent and you are retaining some of your ideal customers, you are losing opportunity (top left). There are still many of your ideal customers who could be more effectively retained with targeted retention efforts.

Finally, if you have deliberate retention efforts focused on your ideal customers, you are thriving (top right). This means you know who your ideal customers are and you are taking specific steps to retain them.

I recently worked with a client who was not practicing purposeful customer retention reduction. The main reason was they did not know who their ideal customer was. They were trying to retain everybody, regardless of whether or not they were the right customer. As a result, their customer base was declining at about 5 percent annually.

Once we clearly identified who their ideal customers were, based on specific segments of the population, they were able to implement specific strategies to retain those customers and even attract new ones. Within a year, the customer base had stopped declining and even grew for the first time in 5 years.

If you assessed yourself in the top right quadrant, congratulations! You have the hardest job of all because you need to stay there. You need to remain focused on your ideal customer and implement specific strategies to attract and retain them.

If you are anywhere other than the top right quadrant, have no fear, you can get there quickly by answering the following questions:

1. What value do we offer to the marketplace? What are our competitive advantages and strengths?
2. Who are our ideal customers? Who would most benefit from what we offer?
3. What deliberate strategies do we need to employ to attract and retain them?

Take a few minutes now to think about those questions, especially the first one.

Until you know exactly whom you are trying to target, you will be wasting effort on those you are not trying to target.

To what extent are you inadvertently losing important customers while retaining unimportant ones?

In order to maximize retention efforts, it is important to know what factors have the greatest influence. The following 10 factors must be built into any growth and retention strategy:

1. Consistency—offering customers the same experience regardless of with whom they speak or where they are
2. Loyalty—creating an emotional connection to your organization and its products and services
3. Innovation—constantly bringing new offerings and ideas to customers
4. Value—offering products and services that meet a customer need, whether real or perceived
5. Quality—offering products and services that meet the quality expectations of your customers

6. Convenience—being easily accessible
7. Prestige—customers feel good about being associated with your organization
8. Service—resolving customer issues quickly and effectively
9. Habit—customers buy from you because it has become a part of their regular routine
10. Benefit—offering real or perceived benefit to customers

How many of these 10 factors are you doing effectively?

Bonus point: Customer satisfaction and service scores are outdated. All they tell you is that you are meeting customer expectations. You cannot build a retention strategy around that. Who cares if customers are satisfied if they do not keep buying from you? What does it matter that the staff is nice if people who browse do not become customers?

One of the key metrics Sleep Country Canada uses to measure customer satisfaction is the conversion rate of shopper to buyer. This is the percentage of people who enter the store and actually buy something.

That is a much better indicator than satisfaction scores and positive feedback.

American Airlines and Customer Disservice

I want to recount for you a recent experience I had with American Airlines, not to pick on AA, but to use it as a case study for what many of you are doing to your customers.

I called American Airlines reservations to book a flight to see a client in Philadelphia. Almost one and a half hours and three ticket agents later, I finally had my ticket booked. The following are some of the particulars with some general questions for you to consider:

The agent I spoke with was in a call centre with other agents, and the background noise was so loud, it sounded like she was in a noisy restaurant. I had to keep yelling my credit card information into the phone.

- Are your employees taking customer calls in a place where they can best focus on the customer?

The travel voucher I was using to book the flight was issued in Canadian dollars, but the AA reservation system only accepts US dollars. It took 20 minutes and three people to figure out how to apply the voucher. Not to mention that it was a paper voucher and needed to be mailed in order to be applied.

- Is your technology or your internal processes limiting your ability to resolve customer issues quickly and effectively?

After all this was completed, I contacted the executive responsible for the customer experience at AA (whose title was SVP of the Customer Experience). I received a voice mail from the Customer Relations department on behalf of this executive, who proceeded to tell me they have no incoming phone lines, so I cannot call them back.

- Are you providing customers an easy way to get in touch with you?

What American Airlines forgot is that every customer complaint is an opportunity to connect with customers. It is an opportunity to help those customers become more loyal. Or even become evangelists for the brand. Had AA handled this properly, I could have become a more loyal customer. Instead, I will avoid using AA at all costs.

Are you providing customer service or doing your customers a disservice?

PROFITABILITY CATEGORY #2

Maximizing Power at the Point of Attack

The most successful organizations are the ones that maximize power on the frontlines of the organization. They attract and hire the right people to begin with, they give their frontline people the power to make decisions (and mistakes), and they are quick to let go poor performers (after giving them an appropriate amount of support and training).

How well does your organization do those three things?

CHAPTER 8

Empowering and Engaging Different Types of Employees to Grow the Business

Every organization has a few different types of employees, but let us simplify and put all of your employees into four groups:

1. Your top performers: These are the employees who perform at an extremely high level and are very successful at what they do. They are essential to the company's success.
2. Your high potentials: These are the employees who perform at a high level and have the potential to perform even better with the right training and support.
3. Your worker bees: These are the employees who are good at what they do and keep the day-to-day business operating. They may have potential for some improvement, but not likely to become high performers.
4. Your cave dwellers: These are the employees who are not very good at what they do, but they have been at their roles for a long time. They have good intentions, but actually end up bringing the organization down.

How do you engage and empower these four types of employees all at the same time? You do not. You treat each type of employee differently, because each of them requires a different level of desired empowerment and engagement.

The first thing you need to do is to try and improve everyone's performance. Look at what your top performers are doing. How are they behaving? What are the behaviors that you would like others to exhibit? Empowerment starts with setting expectation. What do you expect of your employees? How should they behave?

For each of the four types, you need to employ different strategies. For example, you will give your best sales representative more autonomy to make decisions than you give your poorest-performing sales representative. You will give your best customer service representative more tools to resolve customer issues than you will to a poor-performing sales representative. You get what I mean.

I was recently working with a client who wanted to improve the performance of his team and more importantly, reduce the number of times he would be called into customer meetings. I told him that his team members were behaving very differently from each other in the same situations. They were each approaching the issues and opportunities in different ways. However, more importantly, they were not sure how much power they had when working with customers, which was why he was being called into so many meetings.

We needed to show the team what excellence looked like, and what was expected of them. We identified the six behaviors that a top performer in their role would exhibit (things like going into each meeting with a set agenda, calling customers proactively to discuss new service offerings and opportunities, and so on). We developed and implemented tools to support them in better exhibiting those behaviors (coaching, role-plays, tools, and templates). We changed the metrics used to measure their performance by incorporating these new behaviors into their performance reviews.

We immediately saw a change in the way the entire team operated. Conversations with customers improved and became much more proactive and much less contentious. We saw a dramatic improvement in the way the team worked together, sharing success stories and failures to learn from each other. Maybe most importantly, we saw a new level of engagement and empowerment by the team. They took more ownership of their relationships with customers. They owned them. They became more accountable for the organization's success and that which was in the best interests of the customer.

Much of this happened because we showed them what was expected of them and then let them do it. We treated them like adults. Like all teams, this one had employees at different levels of performance. By showing them what excellence looked like, everyone's performance improved. That is what we strive for. Not everyone is going to be a top performer or a high potential, but everyone can make improvements.

Dealing with the Cave Dwellers

A prospective client first mentioned this term, "cave dweller," to describe the people in their organization who were literally hiding out and draining away precious resources. They were no longer an asset to the organization. They were no longer open to change. Their skills and knowledge were either no longer valuable, or no longer worth the drain these people bring to the organization.

By keeping these cave dwellers on the payroll, you send the wrong message to the rest of your organization—that you are willing to tolerate mediocre performance and even abhorrent behavior. Others notice that by doing nothing, you are enabling the behavior. So how do you deal with these case dwellers? You need to draw them out into the light.

You need to set clear expectations for behavior and performance. You need to offer the support and tools and coaching they need in order to improve on those behaviors. You need to measure their contribution differently. Most importantly, you need to move swiftly when you see that they are not willing or capable of performing at the level you expect.

In the example I gave earlier in the chapter, it was clear after 3 months that one of the employees on my client's team was not going to be able to perform at the expected level. She was quickly given a new role within the department—one where she would be able to use her strengths and thrive. Another member of the team decided this role was not for him; so he voluntarily moved to another role. Although these employees were not cave dwellers per se, they were employees who would not have been successful in their roles; so they were swiftly moved to roles where they could add value to the organization.

Take a moment and think as to who your cave dwellers are. Who are those employees who are either bringing the organization down because they refuse to change, or are in the wrong roles? What is it costing you in terms of poor performance or retention or reputation or lost revenue? When you find a cave dweller, you either need to move them to a place where they can be successful or get rid of them. How swiftly you do that will have an impact on the other employees in the organization.

They will thank you for removing the obstacle from their group. They will also see that mediocre performance will no longer be tolerated, forcing them to look for ways to improve their performance.

Empowering and engaging employees in different ways are key to every organization. All of the power cannot be centralized at the top. Your frontline people need to know that you trust them to make smart and critical decisions. If you do not trust them, not only will they know it, but more importantly, why would you put them in roles where they engage with your customers on a regular basis?

If customers are the lifeblood of your organization, why put trolls and cave dwellers on the frontlines as the face of it?

CHAPTER 9

The Champagne Pyramid Concept

Aligning the tactics that your people employ each day with the overall strategy of the organization is like a champagne pyramid at a wedding—it needs to cascade down from the top.

Picture the pyramid of champagne glasses, all set up in perfect rows, piled on top of each other, so that none of them will collapse. When you start pouring the champagne into the glass at the top, it begins to overflow and fill the glasses below it.

Strategy is no different. Strategy needs to be developed at the top of an organization, but everyone else in that organization needs to clearly understand the strategy and their role in it.

The following are some questions you need people in your organization to be asking themselves:

1. Can I articulate in one or two sentences what my organization is trying to accomplish? What are the objectives we are trying to achieve?
2. What is my role in helping us achieve those objectives?
3. How is my performance going to be measured?

If employees in your organization cannot answer these questions well, you can be sure you will not be aligned in what everyone is doing. Of course, everybody means well (or at least most people do). Everyone believes that he or she is doing the right thing in order to make the organization thrive. Nevertheless, if they do not know their role in moving the organization forward (Question #2), then they are going to do what they think is best.

Let us look at each question, so that you can help your employees answer them.

1. Can I articulate in one or two sentences what my organization is trying to accomplish? What are the objectives we are trying to achieve?

When Jack Welch was at GE, his strategy was that he only wanted to operate in markets and industries where GE would be #1 or #2. That provided a very clear direction for the rest of the organization. If you do not think you can be #1 or #2 in your market, then do not go into it.

3M uses the New Product Vitality Index (NPVI) to show the percentage of revenue that comes from products that did not exist 5 years ago. Their internal target for that number is 40 percent. That provides a clear vision to the entire organization that innovation is expected.

Take a few minutes and write down your vision for the organization in two sentences or less. It needs to be clear, concise, and easily communicated.

Here are a couple of examples to get you thinking.

We want to be the number one car company in North America in terms of quality and volume of new car sales, while maintaining a profit margin of at least 10 percent.

With our existing products, we want to grow into new regions that do business in ways similar to that of the markets we are already in.

_____

_____

_____

_____

_____

Let us use the first example given earlier to walk through how this works.

We stated that we want to be the number one car company in North America in terms of quality and volume of new car sales, while maintaining a profit margin of at least 10 percent.

Is that a clear vision? Is it concise? Is it easily communicated? I would say "Yes" to all three. Therefore, we now have a clear vision and objective; so all we need to do is align everything we do with that vision.

2. What is my role in helping us achieve those objectives?

Now that employees know that the organization is trying to be number one in terms of new car sales in North America, their behavior should act accordingly with that. What they are doing on a daily basis should align with that objective.

> Should they be spending time looking at markets outside of North America? No.
> Should they be putting effort into the used car market? No.
> Should they be looking at ways to cut corners on the quality of the vehicles? No.

As a result of this clear vision, employees and managers should be constantly asking themselves, "Will what I am doing help us become number one in North America in terms of quality and number of new car sales?" If done properly, employees will start changing their own behavior as they realize that it does not align with the vision of the organization. That is the ideal state. All you need to do to get there is communicate that clear vision.

Go ahead and try it. Go out and talk with some of your employees. Talk about the vision you identified earlier, and talk to them about what they can do to help achieve it.

3. How is my performance going to be measured?

This is the question in which most organizations mess up. They establish metrics that are inappropriate or unachievable, or they do not communicate them effectively. This is all any employee wants to know, "How are you going to evaluate my performance?" "If I want to get promoted or a raise, what do I need to do?"

Consider the car company example earlier. We need to measure performance based on what is going to help that organization became number one in North America. That means we need to reward the right behavior and discourage the wrong behavior.

> We do not reward mediocre performance because being mediocre will not help us become number one.
> We do not reward dealers who are selling cars at a lesser cost just to increase volumes and meet quotas unless it maintains the 10 percent profitability target.

We do not reward quality departments for compromising quality for speed or volume.

You can see how this works. You develop a clear vision, you communicate it, and every strategy and tactic you employ aligns with it. You should be constantly asking, "Does what we are doing align with where we want to go?"

In the next chapter, we will talk more specifically about setting expectations and measuring the performance of employees to ensure everyone is rowing in the same direction.

CHAPTER 10

Setting the Right Expectations and Measuring Performance

Now that we have a clear vision of the future for our organization (see Chapter 9), and our employees have a pretty good sense of what they can do to help the organization progress toward that vision, we need to set up a more formal way for this to happen. We need to set expectations with each employee and then measure performance based on the expectations we have set.

Let us use two examples from my client work to help illustrate how this can be done.

Example #1: Midsized Medical Device Company

I was recently working with a mid-sized medical device company to help execute their strategic plan. We established a clear vision of the future (growing into two new specific markets). We then needed to translate that vision into action.

I met with the leadership team to develop an implementation plan on how we were going to achieve that vision. The implementation plan consisted of the tactics they needed to employ in order to grow into these two new markets, the person accountable for performing each of those tactics, by when they would be completed, and what would be a successful outcome.

One of the tactics was that we needed to assess the skills and abilities of the sales representatives to sell the products required to help them grow into these new markets. In order to do that, I helped them identify the key behaviors that a top sales rep would exhibit. We came up with seven key behaviors. We then asked each sales rep to assess themselves against these seven behaviors (we asked them to give themselves a score from 1 to 5 on each). We asked their managers to assess them as well.

Once these assessments were complete, we had a strong sense of what training and skills each individual needed, and also areas where the majority of the team was weak and needed more support.

These behaviors helped set expectations. My client was telling the sales representatives about the behaviors they expect the sales representatives to exhibit and that the client would provide them the support to improve their performance in these areas. The behaviors were then built into the performance review for each sales representative and became the foundation for successful growth into these new markets.

Example #2: Large Global Health Care Distribution Company

On this client project, the focus was to work with my client's team to have more proactive discussions with business partners and be considered a strategic adviser to them. The outcome of this would be larger partnership deals, higher fees, and expansion into new services being offered.

Similar to the previous client example, I worked with the client to identify the key behaviors we expected to see. We asked, "What would the characteristics and behaviors of a top-performing person be?" In this case, we came up with five. Some were related to better preparation for meetings with business partners, whereas others were focused on the language to be used and the questions to be asked during meetings with business partners.

I then developed tools for the team to use to help them exhibit the expected behaviors. We role-played specific situations that came up often. We gave them the opportunity to share successes and failure, and more importantly why each situation was a success or failure. We encouraged them to attend each other's meetings when possible and give each other constructive feedback. We even developed a clear value proposition for them to use in meetings.

The results were clear in a short period of time. The fees became higher. The conversations with business partners became less contentious.

The value proposition made its way through the organization so that the CEO was even using it on investor calls. Everyone knew his or her role in helping the organization progress toward its future state.

Again, the keys to success were having a clear future state vision, involving the team in the identification of the key behaviors, clearly communicating what behaviors were expected of them, and measuring their performance (at least partially) based on how they exhibited those behaviors. Therefore, setting expectations and measuring performance is not rocket science. The following is what you need to do:

1. Develop a clear vision for the future.
2. For each department, division, or group of employees, identify the expected behaviors that will help you progress toward that future vision.
3. Integrate those behaviors into performance reviews.
4. Provide tools and support to help employees exhibit the proper behaviors.

It sounds simple, does it not? It is actually simple; it is just not easy. Consider the aforementioned examples and how to replicate that in your own organization.

CHAPTER 11

Determining Your Appropriate Turnover Rate

Employee turnover rate is a metric that all organizations use to determine how well (or how poorly) they keep people employed with their organization. More often, this is measured as employee retention—the percentage of employees who stay.

Turnover rates in most industries tend to be about 15 percent, meaning that 15 percent of employees will leave a company in a given year. Sure, there are differences in the retail industry where seasonal employees are used more frequently, or the resources industry where employees tend to stay for longer so that turnover is lower in most years.

Let us ignore the exceptions on focus on the 80 percent of companies that have a turnover of about 15 percent. Is that a good number? Is it all right to lose 15 percent of your employees every year? I do not know what the right number is (I am sure someone will tell you the right number is 12.34 percent).

What is more important is whether or not you are keeping the employees you want to keep. The employee turnover numbers represent the percentage of overall employees who are leaving a company. Some of those employees should leave. Some should stay. Do you know what your turnover percentage is for employees that you are trying to retain? If it is still 15 percent, then I would be concerned. That means that almost 2 out of every 10 employees you are trying to retain are still leaving. You should be retaining more than 95 percent of the employees you want to keep. It should be an anomaly, not the norm, that one of your top people leave.

In Chapter 7, we discussed *purposeful customer retention reduction*, which meant specifically not trying to retain the customers whom we do not want. The same applies for employees as well. Why are we making retention efforts for employees we do not want? Let them go. Focus your efforts on the ones you do want.

Let us make this more applicable. For starters, how do we measure turnover for those employees we want to retain? Here is an easy way to do that:

Start by identifying who they are. Seriously, go through your organization and identify the 15 or 20 or 200 people whom you really want to retain. Put their names down on a list somewhere. Keep adding to it and taking away from it as new people join the organization or improve their performance or leave. Who should be on this list?

- People who are your top performers in key areas of the organization
- People who have great management and leadership potential
- People who have proven they can adapt to new environments, and learn and apply new skills
- People who take on leadership roles regardless of where they sit in the organization
- People who put the organizations' best interests before their own
- People who can get things done

I think that is a good start for now. Go off and make your list.

You should be focusing your retention efforts on these employees. Get to know them and what they like, and then do everything you can to keep them. And remember that not more than 5 percent of these employees should be leaving in any given year. Why is this important? For two keys reasons: (1) You keep your best people; (2) Every other employee sees that you are making efforts to keep your best people. That means if they want to keep their job, they had better figure out how to be identified as one of those best people.

Not everyone wants to work for a company that is constantly changing and evolving. Not everyone is comfortable with innovation and change. You need to determine what kind of organization you want to be, and then hire and retain the best people to help you achieve that.

Purpose employee turnover means that you are not worried about what percentage of turnover you have for the overall organization, but only for the employees you have identified as critical to the organization's success. Let us assume there are four types of employees in your organization: the top performers, the good performers, the adequate performers, and the poor performers. Here is how I would treat each group:

Group	Retention efforts
Top performers	Very high. You should be offering this group leadership and development opportunities, unique experiences, and levels of responsibility that no one else gets.
Good performers	High. Many good performers may become top performers with training, guidance, mentoring, coaching, and the opportunity to show their abilities.
Adequate performers	Very little. You hope corporate benefits and other general perks are enough to retain the majority of these people. Too high turnover in this area can be very expensive.
Poor performers	None. If they have proven that they cannot improve, then let them go. Do not try and retain them and maybe even let them go.

Your retention focus should be on the top performers, and those good performers who have the potential to be top performers. You should also have a metric to see how you are faring in each of the top two groups. Is your employee turnover rate in the top performers group lower than it is for the overall organization? I sure hope it is. Remember the 95 percent rule. 95 percent or more of these employees should be staying with your organization each year.

Your employee turnover rate should be lower with your top performers than with the rest of the organization. If it is not, then you need to re-evaluate and change your retention strategies. If more of your best people are leaving than the rest of the organization, then you are in trouble.

The obvious benefit of keeping your best people is that you do not have to replace your best people with other people. The following are some other benefits to think about:

- Top people attract other top people. Retaining your best people makes it easier to attract a higher caliber of people.
- Hiring and recruiting costs go down. As you attract more people, you do not have to pay for headhunters or search firms to find you candidates.

- You are investing money in developing people who will have a long-term impact on the organization.
- Your brand and reputation improve.
- Severance costs will go down. Fewer of your top people will want to leave; so you are not forced to pay severance for those wanting to leave.
- Your reputation in the industry goes up. More customers want to buy from you, and more people want to work for you.

By focusing your specific retention efforts on your top people (thus reducing your employee turnover rate with the top two groups), you become the organization that everyone lines up to join, not the one everyone rushes out the door to leave.

Doing the High Jump, Not the Limbo

Organizations need to grow, just like organisms. If you are not growing, then you are declining. You need to focus on raising the bar and going over it, not figuring out ways to lower it and go under. One of the untapped areas is how you develop and implement your best ideas. Unfortunately, not all organizations have a clear way of determining their best ideas. That is where it starts.

The next four chapters will give you strategies on not only how to develop new ideas, but also more importantly, how to make those ideas better and how to maximize the impact of those ideas. What is the point of having a good idea if you cannot maximize its impact? First, let us start with increasing the quality of your ideas.

CHAPTER 12

Increasing the Quality of Your Ideas

Many organizations believe they have great ideas. But how do you determine a good idea from a bad one? We tend to make these decisions in a vacuum. How do I know this? Because we often hear the phrase, "That sounded like a good idea at the time."

We want to ensure that the ideas that we think are good, really are. In many of my group sessions and client meetings, I ask people to rate their organizations on two factors: the quality of their ideas and their organization's ability to implement those ideas.

Look at Figure 12.1. In which quadrant would you put your organization?

Most organizations put themselves in the top left quadrant (quadrant three), meaning they have great ideas but are poor at implementing them.

I always challenge this by saying the reason they put themselves in this quadrant is because their ideas are not as good as they think they are. If the ideas were really that good, they would be easier to implement.

The issue is how people and organizations define what constitutes a good idea. An idea is only a good one if it aligns with the direction that an organization is going, nothing else. Moreover, if an idea aligns with the direction an organization is going, it becomes easier to implement.

The way to get your organization into the top right quadrant is to ensure your ideas and strategies align with the direction of the organization and then become masters of implementation (think back to Chapter 9 and I discuss it more in Chapter 13).

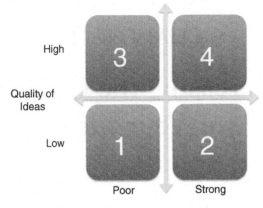

Figure 12.1 Improving the quality of your ideas

We need to realize that there is a difference between a bad idea and poor execution. Not all good ideas work. Some come down to poor execution. Let us talk about two specific examples.

McDonald's Pizza and Target in Canada

A few years ago, McDonald's introduced pizza onto it is menu. We all know that did not work. Let us discuss why. Was it a bad idea or poor execution?

At the time (and mostly still to this day), McDonald's was known for consistency, speed, hamburgers, fries, and chicken nuggets. They were not known for offering a wide variety of fast foods. They were known for offering the same food and the same fast service anywhere in the world. Therefore, when they moved into pizza, it seemed like a logical decision to grow into new product categories. Pizza was a popular fast food category, and McDonald's was trying to capitalize on it.

However, in hindsight, did pizza really fit with McDonald's fast food model at the time? It required an extra 5 minutes of cooking time and required its own oven. This meant more waiting for customers, an investment in new equipment for franchise owners, and less space for the fast food items that had made McDonald's so successful. It turned out to be a bad idea because it never aligned with what had made McDonald's the leading fast food chain in the world.

In 2013, Target decided to move north of the border and open a series of stores in Canada. Similar to the McDonald's pizza idea, within 2 years, the idea was quashed. In this case, it was for different reasons.

Like McDonald's, Target had built a reputation for providing a consistent customer experience in all of its stores. It was logical that Canadians, who would flock to the U.S. to buy at Target, had similar buying habits to Americans, and lived a similar lifestyle, would embrace Target in Canada. However, they did not. Not because it was a bad idea, but because Target botched up the execution.

Moving into Canada did align with Target's strategy for international growth. The problem was that Target did not replicate the customer experience for Canadians. Here are a few reasons why Target is no longer in Canada:

- The prices of the same goods were 20 to 25 percent more expensive in the Canadian stores.
- The product selection was less in Canada, meaning shoppers could not get many of the products they were used to buying at Target in the U.S.
- The supply chain was abysmal, meaning that many products were not on the shelves when customers wanted them.

Target moving into Canada was a good idea, but the execution is what caused it to fail. Target was never able to replicate the same experience it offered in its U.S. stores; so even though there might be a store within 15 minutes of their communities, Canadians would still drive 3 or 4 hours to shop in the U.S. stores.

The next chapter will help you determine what is a good idea and what is a bad idea, without having to wait for hindsight.

CHAPTER 13

Are You Innovative or Opportunistic?

The term innovation tends to be overused, and we punish organizations for not being innovative enough. We automatically assume that all of the most successful organizations are also innovative. However, that is not the case. Some of them are just really good at rapidly and effectively identifying and exploiting opportunities. And there is nothing wrong with that.

What we need to realize is that innovation is important, but it is not the only factor that determines the success of an organization.

We also tend to over-associate innovation with risk. If you take risk, then you are innovative. I am here to tell you that is simply not true. Just because you take risk does not mean you are innovative. Opportunistic companies take risks as well. Of course, it all depends on how you define the term innovation.

My definition of innovation is that an organization is creating a new need (think Sony Walkman or Apple iPod) or creating something that is better than anything else out there.

Being opportunistic means rapidly and effectively identifying and exploiting opportunity.

So what is the most important factor that distinguishes between innovative and opportunistic organization? Approach. Are you proactive or reactive in your approach?

Figure 13.1 shows the two key factors in being innovative—approach and ability to execute. You cannot be innovative if you are not proactive—which you have to be to not only anticipate what is coming, but also to help create it before it happens. You also need to be able to execute. What is the point of being proactive if you cannot get anything done that helps your organization grow?

Figure 13.1 Approach vs. ability to execute

It is important to know where you fit on this chart, but it is even more important to understand where you want to be. Take a moment, think about the strengths of your organization, and write down in which quadrant you would like your organization to be in.

Here are a few characteristics to help you envision where you want to be.

Innovative organizations:

- Embrace productive failure and give employees the freedom to fail
- Build innovation into performance reviews, and they measure the employee's contribution to innovative practices
- Reward behaviors, not just victories
- Formally manage the idea process
- Focus on being proactive and on raising the bar, not solving problems
- Recognize and acknowledge contribution, not just results

Opportunistic organizations:

- Move with agility and speed
- Identify and pounce on new opportunities quickly
- Execute effectively

- Focus on problem-solving and issue resolution—restoring past performance
- Act reactively
- Leapfrog over others who may have gotten there first

No matter whether you are innovative or opportunistic or academic, you need to embrace and exploit it.

Many of you may consider yourselves to be opportunistically innovative, meaning that you are very creative in the solutions you develop to solve problems. My experience is that many organizations would fall into that category.

I often get asked, "How do I become more proactive so I can be more innovative?"

You are not going to like my answer.

You just need to do it. You need to make time every day or every week to think about where your industry is going. Where your organization is going. Where your customer is going. Then think about what impact that will have on your organization. What need you can fulfill.

Many of my clients have told me they hired me because I forced them out of the daily grind of running an organization. I forced them to put the daily firefighting aside and think about the future. That is what you need to do. The following are a few ways that people can find their muse to help them think more proactively:

- Find a trusted adviser (paid or otherwise) to force you to look ahead on a regular basis.
- Join a peer group with non-competitors where the sole purpose of the group is to help each other think ahead and hold each other accountable for doing so.
- Collaborate with an academic organization or think tank that has already done some proactive work that is relevant for your organization.
- Start making bolder predictions about what will happen next in your market.

Therefore, if you are opportunistic and want to become more innovative, it all starts with having a more proactive approach.

If you are an academic organization and want to become innovative, then you need to read the next chapter.

Consider a hockey goalie when a player on the other team is streaking down the wing. The goalie must be proactive by coming out of the net to cut down the angle. If the goalie does not come out, if he is not proactive, the likelihood of the player scoring is higher because they have more of the net to shoot at. By coming out and cutting down the angle, the goalie is forcing the player to react and change his approach, not waiting to see what that player does and reacting to it.

You need to be that goalie. Alternatively, to finish with another hockey reference, Wayne Gretzky, the greatest hockey player of all time, said, "Skate to where the puck is going, not to where it has been."

CHAPTER 14

Identifying
Your *One* Priority

Before we talk about prioritization and executing better on your priorities, we need to ensure that you give yourself and your organization the best chance to succeed. That starts with knowing your ideal future state. Without knowing your ideal future state, you cannot prioritize because you do not know what you are trying to accomplish. In Chapter 9, you started to articulate your ideal future state.

Finding that ideal future state comes down to sitting down as a leadership team or the CEO or President or senior executive of your organization or your business unit or your department and thinking about where you want to be. If we are sitting together 6 or 12 months from now, what does success look like? What does the future bring? Where are you as an organization? What do you want to accomplish? Your ideal future state paints a picture, where you want to get to.

Your vision of the ideal future state needs to be fairly short term. There is no point in making a vision 5 years down the road because you have no idea what the industry is going to look like. You have no idea what your company is going to look like. You have no idea what your customers are going to look like. So make it realistic.

The first question to answer in order to effectively prioritize is, "What is our ideal future state?" This sets the foundation for every decision you make.

Now it is time to identify your one priority. What is the most important priority for your organization? Write in on the line below.

Are you struggling to find just one priority? If so, then you are like most executives and business owners. However, you need to have that one priority, because if you have too many priorities, then you have none.

To help you identify your one priority, consider this question, "What is the quickest and most effective way for me to achieve my ideal future state?" See why it is important to know your ideal future state. Without it, you cannot identify your one priority, which means you cannot prioritize.

My Personal Example

Let me give you a couple of examples to make this real. We will start with me. I am obviously a consultant. I am an expert in operational excellence and work with clients all over the world to help them accelerate growth and find money where they do not normally look. Is that my ideal future state? No, that is what I offer. My ideal future state is helping innovative, exciting, and interesting companies all across the world. That answers the first question.

Then I need to determine, "What is the quickest and most effective way for me to achieve my ideal future state?" I answer the question this way—to raise my profile as a global expert in operational excellence. That is my one priority. Everything I do should be helping to raise my profile as a global expert in operational excellence so I can work with innovative, exciting, and interesting organizations.

If I decide next week that I want to do a teleconference or I decide next month that I want to do a workshop, I must always go back and ask myself if it helps raise my profile as a global expert in operational excellence. If the answer is yes, then I should go ahead and do it. If the answer is no, then I should not. That is figuring out your one priority.

Client Examples

One of the things that my clients tell me almost more often than anything else is that I help them cut through the noise. That I help them realize that things they thought were priorities actually were not.

I recently worked with a client whose executive team had spent well over a million dollars' worth of time and effort discussing an issue that was only going to save them $15,000 to $20,000 a year. All because they did not have their priority figured out. Their one priority was to grow the business, but they were spending endless hours in meetings discussing how to cut costs (and a tiny amount at that). They just needed someone to keep reminding them what was important to the sustainability of the business and take them out of the day-to-day problem solving.

Think about that in the context of your own organization. How much time do you spend talking about things that are immaterial to your organization's ultimate success? It all comes down to prioritization—to asking yourself, "Is what we are discussing going to help us achieve our ideal future state?"

Another client I recently worked with was losing customers at a rate of about 5 percent each year. This is a global organization that has a tremendous reputation and has been around forever. So why were customers leaving? Because my client was trying to be everything to everybody. They had forgotten who their ideal customer was. They stopped trying to meet the needs of the new customers they needed to attract. So what did we do? We identified four key customer segments that provided the fastest and largest opportunity for growth. Then we ensured that all of the strategies we employed, all of the communications we sent out, and all of the marketing plans that we developed would be focused on those four key customer segments.

To summarize, here are the two most important questions when discussing your priorities:

1. What is my organization's ideal future state?
2. What is the quickest and most effective way to achieve that ideal future state?

Think about those two questions before moving on to Chapter 15.

Now try the previous exercise again. What is the most important priority for your organization?

CHAPTER 15

Prioritizing to Maximize the Financial Impact of Your Best Ideas

I am going to assume that you have already read Chapter 14 and have already envisioned your ideal future state. I will also assume that you understand the importance of finding your one priority—the quickest and most effective way to help you achieve that ideal future state. The question I am asked most frequently by my clients or when I do speeches on prioritization is, "What happens when we are already working on three or four priorities and my boss or the parent company in the United States or Europe tells me that there is another priority we need to work on?"

My answer is always the same—if you have too many priorities then you have no priorities. If you are working on too many things, then you cannot move anything forward. Adding new priorities avoids making a decision. The whole point of prioritization is to decide what to spend time and effort on. When organizations refuse to prioritize, or do not know how to do it effectively, it means employees work longer hours and they are more stressed. It hinders performance. More importantly, it is a cop out. It is an organization saying that it will not instill the proper discipline to make decisions that are in the best interest of the customers and the organization. So prioritization by definition is all about identifying what are the most important things for you to work on.

When we talk about prioritization, we talk about your one priority. That one priority has to have a significant impact and that impact is going to be different for every organization. What does impact mean for your organization? Is it purely financial? Reputational? Market share? Employee retention? You have to use certain objective criteria to make the decision. When we really prioritize, we are saying that something is more important than something else. That is why the concept of having multiple priorities makes no sense. One thing will always be more important that the rest.

I could easily argue that my priorities are to live a healthy life, be a good father and husband, and build a successful business. But at some point, I need to determine which one is most important to me. That is my one priority. That is the one thing that will have the greatest impact on helping you progress toward your ideal future state.

Three Key Questions for Prioritization

We have already discussed the first two important questions when it comes to prioritization:

1. What is my organization's ideal future state?
2. What is the quickest and most effective way to achieve that ideal future state?

Once you have asked yourself those two questions, we have to determine what to do if other important things come up. Let us assume that you have identified your ideal future state and your one priority, and then something happens that causes you to possibly rethink that one priority. The market changes. A new competitor enters. Your customer's buying behavior changes. You lose some top people. You get pressure from your boss. How do you deal with that? You have to compare it against your one priority.

This is my third question:

3. Does this new initiative or strategy help us make progress toward our ideal future state faster or more effectively than what we are currently doing (our one priority)?

If the answer is no, then nothing should be done about it. If the answer is yes, then you do not add it as another priority. It becomes your one priority.

This is a very important concept for you all to grasp, because most of your organizations deal in multiple priorities. That is a very ineffective way to run an organization.

Criteria for Prioritization

This third question is a big one and requires some objective criteria to make the decision-making process easier. Here are some criteria you can use to help you prioritize when comparing different initiatives and strategies.

Alignment

It is important that any strategy you implement or any idea you move forward with aligns with your ideal future state. If it does not, then you are wasting your time. This hurdle is a simple yes or no response. "Does the initiative align with the ideal future state?" If the answer is no, then there is no reason to move forward. Why would you put time and effort behind something that is not aligned with the direction you are trying to go?

If the answer is yes, then you start assessing other criteria.

Impact

Impact can be defined differently for each organization. Sometimes impact is purely financial—increased revenues, higher profits, better pricing, lower costs, and so on. However, impact may also be something different. A strategy might have an impact on your customer retention, or reputation as an organization, or your ability to capture investment dollars, or your ability to attract and retain the best people. You need to understand and assess the impact that any new strategy will have. That will help you determine if it helps you achieve your ideal future state more effectively than what you are already doing.

Organizational Capability

When contemplating a new priority, you need to understand what is required to make it happen. Is it going to require hiring a whole bunch of new people? Does it require a whole set of skills you do not currently have? Does it require 12 months for you to implement? All this helps you assess your organization's capability to implement any new initiative you are considering. Look at your organization's capability and consider the following questions:

- Do we have the right people?
- Do we have the right infrastructure?
- Are we able to do this quickly and effectively?
- What will it take to make this happen quickly and properly?

Built into this assessment of organizational capability would also be the concept of speed and whether this accelerates your ability to achieve your ideal future state.

Growth Potential

The last criterion for you to think about is growth potential—whether the new initiative has a greater or lesser growth potential than what you are already working on. Will it open up new markets for you? Is there sustainability to it? If you are considering moving into new markets, do those new markets have a greater growth potential than the markets you are currently in? If you see better growth potential in new markets, you may decide to focus your efforts there, while still maintaining a presence in your current markets.

Therefore, the third important question, which really gets to the heart of prioritization, is:

Does any new initiative or strategy that we are considering help us make progress toward our ideal future state faster or more effectively than what we are currently doing (our one priority)?

Without asking this question, you are never going to be able to effectively prioritize what gets worked on, because every decision will be made in a vacuum.

PROFITABILITY CATEGORY #4

Taking Procurement Out of the Basement

The title of this section came from my work with hospital clients. When I visited my clients, many of whom were CFOs and senior procurement people, their offices were often in the basement of the hospital. I would need to go through unpainted corridors to find a small office with a few people packed into it. In one case, the procurement office was next to the morgue.

Is that the way to treat the people responsible for helping the organization purchase millions of dollars of goods and services? We need to take procurement out of the basement. We need to realize the value that procurement can offer to the organization. It is a support service, not a compliance function. It is run by smart people who know how to build relationships and negotiate contracts, not gnomes who stamp purchase orders.

By changing how you look at the procurement function in your organization, you can completely change the results it achieves. Sure, cost savings are important, and so is getting the best price for all of the commodities you buy. However, the right procurement people can add so much more value. They can better leverage the assets you already pay for. They can build stronger relationships with suppliers and business partners. They can create more value through contractual relationships. They can create better return on investment from your purchases. Is not that worth investing in?

CHAPTER 16

Turning Procurement Operations into a Revenue Generator

Procurement is a funny thing because it is often thought of as a compliance function. In most organizations, the procurement department reports into the finance department and is not given a lot of strategic responsibility.

Well, that is about to change. Procurement can be a strategic function in your organization if you structure it properly. It starts with making a clear distinction: There is a difference between commoditized and strategic procurement.

Commoditized procurement is buying things that are not essential to the success of your organization and where there are many options. Think pens and office supplies, and printers, copiers, and computers.

Strategic procurement is buying things that can have a profound impact on the success of your organization. Think consulting, technology, and advisory services.

The purpose of an effective procurement department is to make the distinction between these two types of procurement and add value accordingly. In commoditized procurement, the value is in finding the lowest price for an acceptable product or service. Because it is a commodity, there will be many viable options; so getting the lowest price for an acceptable level of quality makes sense.

For strategic procurement, cost should be one of the last considerations. Do you want the cheapest consultant or accountant or technology system? No. Procurement departments can add value here by advising the organization on the best method for making the right decision—helping to determine the right decision-making criteria, the right people to make the decision, and the right focus and weight of the different criteria.

Commoditized procurement is about cost. Strategic procurement is about outcomes and value. So how does this help us to generate revenue through our procurement department?

Figure 16.1 shows the key factors in making your procurement function a revenue generator—power and value.

Give yourself a score from 1 to 10 on how much power your procurement department has within your organization. A lot of power would mean that procurement can stop anyone from buying something, has a strategic seat at the executive table, and can influence the margins of your organizations. A little amount of power means that procurement is not taken seriously, bypassed during the buying process, and each individual department does its' own buying.

Now give yourself another score of 1 to 10 on the value that your procurement department provides. A high-value department would formally manage key supplier relationships, act as a business partner to the other departments in the organization, leverage current purchased assets, and focus on getting the best return for the organization's purchasing dollars. A low-value department would focus on the lowest price, frustrate

Figure 16.1 Procurement as a revenue generator

suppliers and employees, and default to policies and procedures over good judgment.

If your procurement department has little power and offers little value, it actually erodes your margins. It means you are paying people who have no influence in decision making and offer no value. They do not enhance what you are doing.

If the procurement department has a lot of power, but it is not providing a lot of value, then it is acting merely as a compliance officer. At this point, your procurement people can say "No" but they cannot say "Yes." They are merely enforcing the rules your organization has put in place and are not questioning whether those rules make sense and are not supporting the rest of the organization in making those rules work for them.

If your procurement department offers a lot of value but has little power, then you are missing opportunities. You have people who can add value and can help the organization make better decisions, but you are not providing them with the ability to do so. Their abilities are wasted because they have no influence.

If your procurement department has a lot of power and offers high value, it can have a significant impact on your bottom line. Your procurement people support the organization to help them make better purchasing decisions. They build strong relationships with key partners. They implement policies that make sense and change them when they do not.

The more value the procurement department offers, the more it can help the organization's top line. The following are a few ways in which that can happen:

- Helping the organization select a solution in the best interests of the customer, thus helping with customer retention
- Selecting strategic business partners who will collaborate with your organization to make performance improvements
- Reducing the administrative burden on the rest of the organization (especially sales reps) to free them up to do their jobs—finding new sources of revenue

Turning your procurement department into a revenue-generating one can be done. However, you need to structure it properly and set it up for success.

You need to **hire people with a service mindset,** as they will be supporting the entire organization. They will have lots of internal customers.

You need to put **guidelines** (not policies or procedures) in place that allow your other departments to have some flexibility in their purchasing decision making.

You need the procurement department to **report to a senior executive with some strategic responsibility** across the organization. They need to be given the power to influence important buying decisions.

You need to **formally manage relationships with key suppliers.** Most organizations do not effectively manage the contracts and service levels they have in place with key suppliers. This just saps value (and margins) out of the organization. Regular performance reviews and discussions on achieving mutual objectives will go a long way in building stronger relationships with key business partners.

They need to provide **strategic advice.** Procurement people should be experts on how to buy things and how to get the best return on investment on purchasing dollars. Too often, procurement acts as a gatekeeper and compliance officer, focusing on policies and procedures and finding the cheapest solution. Work with internal departments and act as a strategic partner to help them get what they want, not a police officer scrutinizing their every move.

You need to use **different metrics for success.** Procurement departments should not be measured based only on the amount of savings achieved. That promotes the wrong behavior (cost cutting). When you look at more strategic metrics—percentage of purchasing dollars spent on new innovations, average profit margin per procurement employee, percentage of key suppliers being formally managed, and the amount of spend under management—it encourages different behavior from your procurement department.

You need to **anticipate needs.** The most valuable procurement departments anticipate what their customers (the other internal departments) need and help figure out the quickest and most effective ways to meet those needs. They do not wait for departments to come to them, they proactively reach out.

You can do all of these things; you just need to decide how you want your procurement department to be run.

CHAPTER 17

Managing Supplier Relationships and Service Levels Effectively to Increase Profits

You spend hours and hours building strong relationships with your suppliers and business partners. You spend even more hours negotiating favorable contracts with those suppliers and business partners. You want better pricing, more value, longer support hours, newer technology—anything to make you feel good about the relationship.

Then what do most organizations do? They move on to the next fire that needs dousing or the next issue that needs resolving.

Managing your supplier relationships is one of the quickest and easiest ways to increase your profitability. I guarantee you are losing money, either directly or indirectly, through the poor management of your suppliers. Do not feel bad. Everybody does it. There is nothing sexy about managing supplier relationships. It is not the same as closing a new sale or bringing on a new customer or opening up in a new market.

However, let us take an example of how important it can be. A client of mine, the chief executive officer (CEO) of a large hospital, told me that every Saturday he would get calls from his emergency room (ER) nurses telling him that there were not enough supplies on the cart in the ERs. This meant that while a patient was in the ER, nurses would spend valuable time looking for supplies in the various storage closets around the hospital instead of dealing with the patient.

When my client went to his supplier, the supplier showed him all of the on-time delivery metrics, which showed that the product was getting to the hospital in plenty of time to be put on the carts. Once we dug a little deeper, we realized the supplier was measuring on-time delivery to the shipping doors of the hospital, not to the actual place where the product was needed (it was the supplier's responsibility to get the products on the cart).

For months, this issue had gone unnoticed and unresolved because my client was not managing the supplier relationship effectively enough. The contract clearly stated that on-time delivery was to be measured *to the cart* (not to the shipping door). The supplier had been measuring it improperly for months.

This error in measuring cost the hospital thousands of dollars in rush orders as well as hundreds of hours of wasted time by its nurses.

So how do you avoid this situation?

1. Stratify your supplier relationships. See Figure 17.1 as an example of how to do this. Go through each of your suppliers and assign them a Tier. This then determines how you will interact with them on a regular basis.
2. Meet regularly with Tier 1 and Tier 2 suppliers to not only discuss issues, but also to ensure your objectives are aligned and the metrics show progress on those shared objectives.
3. Sign contracts that are no longer than 3 to 5 years in most cases. Technology is changing so quickly that most ideas are obsolete in 5 years. Give yourself the opportunity to see what else is out there.

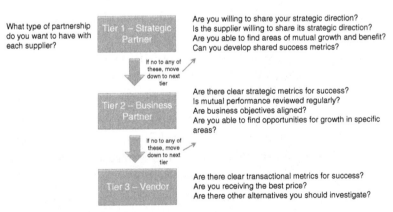

Figure 17.1 Stratifying your supplier base

4. Ensure that you get all key contracts, renewals, amendments, and extensions in writing. You never know who may leave your company or who may need to review the information. It gives you the ability to better manage what was promised in the contract.

5. Agree upon clear service levels and then manage them. This provides a clear picture on what the supplier needs to deliver on. Consider what is really important and remember my client example from earlier—is it important to know that the product arrived at the shipping door or that it got onto the cart where it is needed?

In summary, this chapter tells you to better manage the relationships you have with your suppliers. Find mutual objectives in order to stay in synch. Have regular meetings to not just discuss issues and past results, but also future ideas and ways to improve the working relationship. Manage the service levels, and collaborate on ways to improve that performance.

It is not rocket science, it just takes discipline and the right mindset in order to capture all the value you can from your supplier relationships.

The TAO of Cost Minimization

The word TAO (Theft, absenteeism, and obsolescence) means so many things to so many people. In this case, we are talking about how to find your organization's inner peace around minimizing costs—minimizing the costs of making your product; minimizing the cost of employees not showing up to work; and minimizing the cost of theft and obsolescence. These are all ways that your organization bleeds money. Cost cutting will never be the focus of a thriving organization, but cost control, avoidance, and minimization are important components of any profitable business.

CHAPTER 18

Minimizing Theft, Absenteeism, and Obsolescence in Your Organization

Money seeps out of your organization in many ways. Theft, absenteeism, and obsolescence (TAO) are three of those ways. You will notice that one way to reduce all three is by empowering employees and making them feel a part of the organization. Treat them as owners of the organization. However, let us look at how to tackle each of the ways individually.

Theft

Although you may not think theft as a problem, it is. It can be called shrinkage or loss prevention or many other names, but it is a problem. It is such a big problem that most organizations actually budget for it, as yours may do. Just think about that for a minute. You budget for the fact that 5 to 10 percent of the products you make will disappear for various reasons. According to Retail Knowledge, customer and employee theft cost the retail industry more than $60 billion in 2015 in the U.S. alone. That is a staggering number. Do you do anything to stop it?

The single most effective way to stop employee theft is to empower your employees to take ownership and accountability for their work. If people feel empowered, important, and acknowledged, they will take fewer things from the organization. If they are really passionate about what they do and are loyal to the company, stealing from the organization would feel like stealing from themselves. Not only will they not do it, they will also stop others from doing it.

I know it sounds crazy, but making your employees feel good about their work and proud about their company will significantly reduce your shrinkage.

The following are some ways for you to tackle employee theft specifically:

- **Measure your inventory**. You should be doing this anyways in order to control your inventory costs, but manage your inventory. You should be able to track what is coming in and what is going out and what is being stored. Once you reconcile that, you can see if anything is missing.
- **Keep an organized workplace and warehouse**. Everything should have a place. When products are strewn all over the place, it looks like no one is keeping track. That encourages the, "no one will miss it" mindset. If you cannot keep your facilities clean and organized, it will impact how your employees act.
- **Connect the dots**. Let them know that stealing from you is the same as stealing from themselves. The more products go missing, the higher the costs for the organization. The higher the costs, the lower the profits. The lower the profits, the less money for investment in salaries, employee development, and financial incentives.

Absenteeism

According to multiple sources, including Statistics Canada, the average employee in North America misses almost 10 days of work per year. If you consider that there are about 200 workdays in a year, it means employees miss about 5 percent of work each year. That may not sound like much, but do you know how much that is costing you? Overall, it is costing North American businesses tens of billions of dollars each year.

The best companies have an absentee rate of closer to 6 days per year. That is a 40 percent difference. That should get your attention.

Let us put together an example of what this might mean. Let us say we have two companies that are the same size—$300 million in revenue with 200 employees. The average salary per employee is $50,000 (or roughly $250 per day per employee). Company A employees average 10 days per year in absenteeism and Company B employees only miss an average of 6 days owing to absenteeism (which is where the best in class organizations fall into).

Company A

200 employees missing 10 days each = 2,000 missed days per year at $250 per day = $500,000

The cost of absenteeism is $500,000 per year

Company B

200 employees missing 6 days each = 1,200 missed days per year at $250 per day = $300,000

The cost of absenteeism is $300,000 per year

Company A is spending roughly $200,000 more than Company B on employees who are doing no work. More importantly than the cost is the fact that Company A is losing 800 more days of productive employee work. How will they make up for that lost work? What is not getting done as a result of those lost days? How much are they falling behind on customer orders or acquiring new customers as a result of those lost days?

Now are you convinced yet that this needs to be dealt with?

The following are some ways to reduce absenteeism:

- **Treat employees as owners**. I know I mentioned it as it relates to theft, but it also relates to absenteeism. If your employees are passionate about what they do and are loyal to your organization, they will want to come to work. Moreover, they will feel guilty about missing work.
- **Track attendance**. Every semester, on my kids' report card, we see how many days they were absent. This helps us determine if they have skipped any school. You do not need

role calls or punch cards or to formally take attendance, but figure out a way to track whether or not people are working.

- **Give some options.** If someone is sick and cannot come in the office, can they still be productive working from home? Can they call in to the important meeting instead of being there in person? Sometimes things happen that we cannot control and the more options you provide to still get work done, the less likely it will be for employees to miss work. If I have to stay home to take care of a sick child, that does not mean I cannot be productive.

Obsolescence

I will refer you back to Chapter 12 when I talked about increasing the quality of your ideas. If you are gathering ideas from employees and customers, suppliers and business partners, if you are aware of what is going on in the marketplace, if you build an environment that is constantly challenging the status quo, then becoming obsolete is not a concern.

Blackberry became obsolete because it overestimated the value of data security with consumers.

Fuji became obsolete because it failed to notice the shift in customer behavior toward wanting more digital pictures.

Blockbuster became obsolete because it failed to react to new competitors who were offering a better, faster, and a more convenient movie-watching experience.

There are thousands of examples of companies that became obsolete because they stopped learning and they stopped innovating. They became too comfortable in their environment and stopped noticing what was going on around them.

PROFITABILITY CATEGORY #6

Supply Chain Optimization

There are many different components to a supply chain, starting with finding raw materials to make products and ending with the end of a product's life. In between, there is manufacturing and inventory management, distribution and defect management, and product returns. All of these functions are often considered to be necessary costs in the supply chain. But what if you could turn them into revenue generators?

Don't you agree that optimizing your product returns process cannot only save you money, but also become a competitive advantage? What if you stopped worrying about fighting customers on returns and just accepted them all? It would open up a completely new world of opportunities for you around loyalty and brand reputation.

Most organizations do not think that way because they are more concerned with the burden that returns pose. What if you could think the same way about waste or defects? What if you could reduce the number of touch points in your supply chain? Or turn your distribution network into a competitive advantage?

The next four chapters will educate you about the different possibilities around cost minimization and also how to exploit some of the necessary components of your business for revenue growth.

CHAPTER 19

Profiting from Returns, Defects, and Waste

There are many operational challenges that we think about as just the costs of doing business. When you sell products, sometimes customers are going to want to return them. When you manufacture products, sometimes you will make mistakes and build defective ones. Any time we need to hand off a product or information to someone else, we create waste. So why bother writing this chapter? Because in case you had not guessed by now, it is all about the way you approach these "costs of doing business." Are they burdens or opportunities?

Finding the right balance between speed, cost-effectiveness, and quality is a lost art. We often see organizations chasing one or two without considering the others.

Blackberry came to market with its Playbook tablet too soon. It focused purely on speed to market and not quality or cost-effectiveness. The tablet was of poor quality and over-priced. Blackberry eventually needed to drop the price in order to sell off its inventory.

According to a CapGemini Consulting study, about 90 percent of companies admit that they are too slow to market (from the e-book *The Innovation Game: Why and How Businesses are Investing in Innovation Centers*); so the majority of organizations are not focusing enough on speed to market, even though they may be focused on quality and cost-effectiveness.

Microsoft launched the Zune device to compete with Apple's iPod. The only problem with that was that the Zune was a clearly inferior device. The screen often froze. It was not as user-friendly as the iPod and did not have a sufficient music store interface. Because of its poor quality,

Microsoft lost hundreds of millions of dollars through the development and advertising of the Zune device.

You need to strike a balance between these three factors (speed, quality, and cost-effectiveness) when you bring a product to market. It makes the returns process smoother and reduces the number of defects you will manufacture.

The Returns Process

Unfortunately, not every customer who buys something from you wants to keep it. The good news is that how you treat returns can help you not only improve customer loyalty but also grow your business. A stringent return policy dissuades customers from buying from you. If a customer is not happy and knows they have to jump through layers of bureaucracy to return the product, they are less likely to buy it in the first place. That is just human nature.

However, if you have a liberal return policy, you will increase the likelihood of someone buying your product. Even if they just want to try it. And those that try if often end up keeping it. You also create a stronger bond with your customer. The customers know that they can return something and not be hassled; therefore, they will likely come back and buy more from you. They are very likely telling their friends about the experience they had with you, which leads to more customers buying from you. Can you see how this works?

I mentioned in a previous chapter that any time a customer interacts with your organization in any way, you have an opportunity to win or lose their loyalty. Returns are no different. Make it hard and they will stay away, and make it easy and they will come back regularly.

Zappos has one of the more liberal return policies out there. It allows you to print a prepaid shipping label from the website in order to send your return back. Not only do you have 365 days to return the product, Zappos will pay for the shipping of your returned product as well. It is no coincidence that Zappos has one of the most engaged and loyal customer bases.

Ikea, the Swedish furniture seller, has a take-back program in Sweden and France. When customers buy new furniture, Ikea will take back the old furniture and either resell it as used furniture or recycle the materials. This not only creates loyalty with existing customers because they can return the furniture when they are finished with it, but it also creates a new customer base who might not be able to afford new furniture, but can afford used furniture at a discounted price. I would expect that it would not be long before we see this same take-back program in Ikea stores in North America.

Another reason why you want to make your returns process easy is that it helps you collect data. What products are being returned? Why are they being returned? Do they come from certain geographies more than others? Certain stores? Certain locations? This information can help you identify issues in production, ebbs and flows in demand, and perception of the quality of your product. All of these will help you anticipate what products customers will want.

Bet you never associated your returns process with better customer retention and higher profits. Well, now you can.

Defects and Waste

Defects and waste are usually associated with manufacturing organizations. "We need to minimize defects and eliminate waste!" Hence the creation of Lean and Six Sigma and many other methodologies that should go the way of the dinosaur.

At this point, I could tell you about my manufacturing client who had scrap metal waste left over from the production of their goods and sold that scrap metal to a third party. That was pretty creative.

Or I could tell you about another client who trained most of their production line workers on quality standards so that defects could be avoided altogether or caught before the product became a finished good. That was pretty innovative as well.

I would prefer to talk about the future of manufacturing, because that is much more important and much more relevant. Most manufacturing organizations have similar technologies and methodologies that allow them to minimize defects and waste. What most of them do not have is a strategic view of where the manufacturing industry is going. So I am here to provide it.

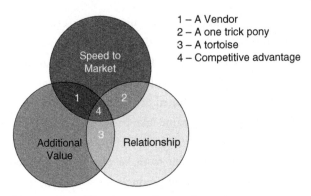

Figure 19.1 The future of manufacturing

The future of manufacturing will not be in cost cutting and eliminating waste. It will be increasing speed to market (or decreasing lead times), providing additional value to customers, and building stronger relationships. Figure 19.1 shows the relationship between these three elements.

If you have speed to market and provide additional value, but have poor relationships with customers, you are a vendor. Customers think of what you offer as a commodity and will not show much loyalty.

If you have speed to market and a strong customer relationship, but add no additional value, then you are a one-trick pony. Customers love you because you are fast, but they will not view you as a partner. When they need additional support, they will go elsewhere.

If you provide additional value and have a strong customer relationship, but do not have speed to market, you are a tortoise. You might win the race once in a while because customers like you and are loyal to you, but as soon as they need something faster, customers will run from you.

When you have speed, provide value, and have strong relationships, you have a competitive advantage. You have the loyalty you need, the speed to keep customers happy, and the additional value to encourage them to keep coming to you for additional support.

That is the future of manufacturing. If you get caught up in the race around manufacturing technology, good luck.

Relationships with the customer, the customer experience, how fast you move, and the perception customers have of the value you bring will always win out in the long run over shiny, new technology.

CHAPTER 20

Leveraging Your Supply Chain to Generate Profits

Twenty years ago, we used the word "Logistics" to describe everything in a supply chain. I am sure this came from the military that used Logistics departments to manage the replenishment of supplies to the troops. More recently, we started calling it a "supply chain," because we were moving goods along a chain to get to a final destination.

During this transition in terminology, we also became more sophisticated in how supply chains were operated and managed. We went through a period where offshoring was the only way to operate—contracting out manufacturing to those countries where the labor costs were lower. Then we realized that having our products made halfway around the world poses some challenges, not the least of which were management of the contract manufacturer and lead times getting the products to the end customers. Therefore, we began onshoring and nearshoring.

We developed concepts like just-in-time (JIT) and on-demand manufacturing to reduce inventory and customize products. Dell was one of the best examples of this. Fifteen years ago, you could go to the Dell website and create a customized computer that would be assembled and delivered within a few days—a novel concept at the time. Does anyone still use that Dell website to build their own computer? Not many, because personal computers have taken a back seat to other personal devices and we realized that most out-of-the-box computers have more than enough features to satisfy us.

Supply chain management goes through different variations and concepts, but there are a few absolute rules about the supply chain.

Absolute rule #1: The more a product is moved and the longer the lead time, the more your profit margins will erode. Every time you touch a product, it costs you money. The longer you store a product, the more it costs.

Absolute rule #2: The more you empower employees to build quality products, the more quality products you will sell. The concept of having quality control at the end of a manufacturing process makes no sense. What if you could have identified the quality issue earlier on?

Absolute rule #3: The faster you can deliver on a quality product, the more value it has to your customer. Going back to Figure 19.1, speed to market is a competitive advantage, as long as it is coupled with a quality product.

Note: Quality should be defined as meeting or exceeding customer expectations, not meeting some arbitrary standard.

Absolute rule #4: Sharing information and using it effectively is critical to anticipating and meeting demand. I call this *applied wisdom*. There is no shortage of companies losing money because products that customers wanted were not available or that use information incorrectly. There are also many companies that collect the wrong data or too much, and then get overwhelmed trying to translate that data into something useful.

Absolute rule #5: The longer a product sits in inventory, the lesser value it has. I have worked with companies where some products have become obsolete because they were lost in a warehouse or the turnover was too slow.

When you are evaluating your supply chain or building one from scratch, you need to remember these absolutes. They will form the foundation of a supply chain that focuses on value, speed, and getting the product in the hands of your customers.

To put them differently, you need to:

- Minimize the number of touch points in your supply chain;
- Empower employees to take accountability for the quality of the product;
- Ensure you provide speed to market;
- Use information effectively; and
- Get your inventory out of your warehouse as quickly as possible.

Follow these five absolutes and you will have a supply chain that makes you money, not one that costs you money.

CHAPTER 21

Reducing the Number of Touch Points in Your Supply Chain

If you know the story of King Midas, you will know that everything that King Midas touched turned to gold. That is how your supply chain should function. At every step in the supply chain, your product should turn to gold. Or put a different way, you need to have *touchpoint leverage*. When you have touchpoint leverage, every step in a process, every interaction with a customer, and every part of your supply chain process adds value. You are not just assembling something, you are enhancing it.

A typical product will go through the following steps (and others in many cases):

1. Raw materials are sourced from a location.
2. Those raw materials are moved to a production facility.
3. They are stored in the production facility (maybe even many production facilities).
4. They are combined with other materials to make a finished or unfinished product.
5. If unfinished, the product is then combined with other materials to make a finished product.
6. The finished product is then reviewed to ensure its quality.
7. The finished product is stored in the production facility or moved to another storage location.
8. It is packaged with other finished products for shipment.
9. The packaged product is moved onto a trailer for transportation to another location or directly to the customer.

I have significantly oversimplified this process to show the steps involved. I did not factor in cross-docking, off-shoring, products being manufactured at multiple locations, or products where additional packaging or labeling is required.

Are you confident that your supply chain is adding value at every step of the aforementioned process?

Let us look at some questions we can ask ourselves to ensure of this:

- In step 1, are we sourcing materials from locations close to our production facility? This will reduce transportation and storage costs.
- In steps 3 and 4, are we combining materials in the proper order? This will help with the flow of goods.
- In step 6, why wait until the product is finished to ensure its quality? Toyota revolutionized the quality process by allowing workers to stop the line when they saw a defect. I do not think this is the right process, but waiting until you have used your full resources to build a product only to find it is a defect is a waste of money and resources.

I am sure you have come up with many ideas of your own on how to improve this process. Do you do the same thing with your own supply chain?

You need to consider how to add value at each step. Think outside the box. Question each step of the process.

Can the raw materials be brought right into the production facility and used right away?

I worked for McCain foods plant in a small town named Harnes in northern France. This particular plant made French fries; so potatoes were the essential ingredients. The plant was located in Harnes because there were potato farms all around the surrounding areas. Each morning, farmers would line up with their trucks filled with potatoes and those potatoes would go right on to the production line to be used. This not only reduced storage costs for the raw materials, but also reduced spoilage of the potatoes and put the onus on the farmers to bring the potatoes fresh to the plant.

Can the product be moved from the production line right to the trailer for transport to the customer?

A manufacturing client of mine had the production line end near the shipping doors. Once the product was finished, it would be piled up and immediately loaded onto the truck for transport. Once the truck was full, it would leave with the finished product and another would take its place. Again, this cut down on storage costs and shortened the lead time in getting the product to the end customer.

Think of yourself as the King Midas of supply chains. Your job is to ensure that every step in your supply chain enhances the value of the products you are selling.

CHAPTER 22

Lowering Inventory by Anticipating Demand

Inventory management is all about information. How much product is being stored? Where is it being stored? When will it be moved? The way to lower inventory, and make more money, is to do your best to anticipate demand to minimize inventory, and with the inventory you do have, get it out to the end customer as quickly as possible.

With all of the tools that we have today, anticipating demand should be easy. The problem is, we have so many tools and data, how do you know what to use?

Organizations are being fed constant information through a variety of channels. You need a framework to determine what information to act upon and what information to ignore. During a speech, I told a group of executives that there were only three factors in determining whether or not the information you were getting was useful. Those factors are impact, alignment, and feasibility.

Impact means that acting upon the information will provide a benefit to your organization. That benefit can be financial, increase in your reputation, or help you attract and retain ideal customers.

Alignment means that acting on the information aligns with your overall corporate strategy. It will help you move closer to your ideal future state.

Feasibility means that it is actually possible to act upon the information. You can actually do something with it.

Only when all three of these factors are present, does it make sense to act upon information to reduce your inventory. See Figure 22.1 to help explain why.

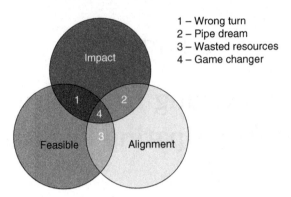

Figure 22.1 Finding useful information

If acting upon the information you have gathered is feasible and can have an impact, but does not align with your corporate direction, then you are taking a wrong turn. You are going in the wrong direction.

If acting upon the information can have an impact and aligns with your corporate direction, but is not feasible, then it is a pipe dream. There is nothing material you can do with the information.

If acting upon the information is feasible and aligns with your corporate direction, but will have no impact, you are wasting resources.

When you have all three, it is a game changer.

A friend of mine started a point-of-sale business that he ended up selling to a large retail information management company. His technology provided real-time point-of-sale information to his customers (who were smaller retail stores and chains). This information told them who was buying what, when, and where. Now this information is available in most retail solutions; so what was different about his solution?

It was not about the information he was gathering, it was about how the information was used. He would work with each of his customers to determine what information would be useful for them and filtered out the rest. The other information was still available to them, but only if they requested it. He started by asking them what information would help them run their business more effectively and why they wanted the information. Effectively, he asked them the outcome they wanted from using the data so that he could provide the most useful data to them.

The companies that successfully used the data to improve their inventory management were able to do so because they asked for data that helped achieve their objectives. It helped them determine where certain products were purchased most frequently. It helped them determine which days of the week were the busiest and which the slowest. It helped determine if customers were buying certain types of clothing during certain times in the day. This real-time information was used to ensure that the right products were on the shelves at the right times.

These successful companies were able to better anticipate demand for their products by effectively using data to understand their customers' buying habits.

Are you effectively using data to anticipate and fulfill customer needs?

Here is a short self-assessment to help you determine the answer to that question. Rank yourself from 1 to 5 on these questions, with 1 being the lowest and 5 being the highest.

1. We look at the outcome we want to achieve before determining what data to use.
2. We track our customers' buying habits.
3. We accurately track all inventory.
4. We rarely have stock-outs or product shortages.
5. All the data we track have a specific purpose.

The highest score you can get is 25. The most successful companies will score 20 or higher. If you scored 10 or less, you need to address your use of information. It is likely you are tracking the wrong information, or using the right information improperly.

The following are some ways to increase your score (and manage your inventory better):

- Determine what outcomes you want from the information and then determine what information will help you achieve them.

- Look for patterns in the way that your customers buy and look ahead to the future. What future events will impact how your customers make purchases?
- Focus on increasing your number of inventory turns. There are specific strategies you can employ to get your inventory turning faster.

Anticipating demand can help you lower your inventory levels and maximize your performance and profitability. It all starts with determining what outcomes you want and determining the best information to help you achieve them.

PROFITABILITY CATEGORY #7

Operational Excellence

In my first book, *Redefining Operational Excellence*, I wrote that operational excellence is a mindset, not a methodology. I have never believed that more firmly than now. The old ways of operational excellence are dying. Trying to apply Lean or Six Sigma to commercial processes does not have any sustainable results. The whole premise is wrong because those methodologies assume each customer is the same and each situation is the same. We all know that it is not true.

Operation excellence needs to focus on helping an organization thrive. A thriving and valuable operational excellence function will help the organization generate revenue, attract and retain customers, identify and implement new ideas, become more innovative, and maximize profitability. If your operational excellence function is not doing that, then you are doing something wrong.

There are four key components to building a thriving operational excellence practice in your organization.

1. **Act like King Midas**. As the rap group Run DMC once sang, *"Just like King Midas, as I was told, everything that he touched, turned to gold."* Everything the operational excellence department touches should turn to gold. The job of an operational excellence department is to make the organization better, not just to support it.

2. **Lead Them Through the Tunnel**. Too many operational excellence departments believe their role is to go into other departments as an extra set of hands, and disrupt the way they operate or tell them how to do things better. That is not its purpose at all. A thriving operational excellence function shows the organization the light on how to better prioritize so that only the best strategies and ideas are

being worked on. It shows the other departments the right tools to use so that those departments can thrive on their own, without being reliant on someone else. A thriving operational excellence function teaches everyone else in the organization how to achieve their own level of excellence.

3. **Be the Fountain of Youth for Ideas**. A thriving operational excellence function is the constant source of new ideas and new opportunities. It helps make the intrinsic extrinsic by identifying best practices and key pieces of information and figuring out how to share and replicate it across the organization. It also helps stimulate the thinking of others. The operational excellence function should not always be the source of the ideas, but definitely can be the catalyst for helping others come up with them.

4. **Be a Jack of All Trades and Master of All of Them**. An operational excellence department needs to prod, poke, and provoke. It needs to be part strategic adviser, part therapist. Part provocateur and part voyeur. It needs to see things differently and provide new insights and perspectives. It needs to challenge the status quo and take people out of their comfort zones to find better solutions.

How does your operational excellence function stack up in those four areas?

The next five chapters will show you how changing your mindset about operational excellence will help you identify and exploit opportunities in a different way.

CHAPTER 23

Finding Profit Increases in Areas You Do Not Normally Look

The key to operational excellence is an area where innovation, performance, and true profit intersect. When you enter that sweet spot, it becomes much easier to exploit opportunities. The key is figuring out how to get there.

Innovation is not just about coming up with new ideas; it is also about how successful you are at implementing those ideas.

Performance is about how good you are at exploiting new opportunities.

True profit means that you are maximizing profitability.

In other words, finding the sweet spot in operational excellence happens when you are able to maximize the impact of your best ideas, you are able to exploit your best opportunities, and you are able to maximize profitability. Figure 23.1 shows how these three factors intersect.

If you have innovation and strong performance, but are not achieving true profit, then you are leaving money on the table.

If have innovation and are maximizing profit, but have weak performance, then you are hanging by a thread. The success you are enjoying may not last long.

If you have strong performance and are maximizing profit, but have no innovation, you are dying a slow death. Others will catch up and surpass you.

When the three converge, you are a thriving organization that is pursuing operational excellence. In addition, the way to find money where others do not normally look is to find areas of the organization where one

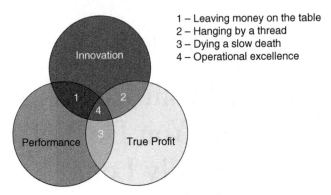

Figure 23.1 Finding operational excellence

of the three factors is missing and then exploit them. Where is innovation lacking? Where are you unable to maximize the value of your ideas? Where do you know, intuitively, that you are leaving money on the table? Where are you concerned about how slowly you jump on new opportunities?

The following are some examples I have seen with my clients:

- A highly profitable product that has not been changed or updated in a long time and new competition had entered the marketplace.
- A revolutionary new device that had some success, but is thought of around the organization as a commercial failure.
- A process that requires so many approvals that things never get signed off.
- A customer onboarding process that is so cumbersome that more than 10 percent of customers decide to go elsewhere once it begins.
- A customer response process so administrative that detailed price quotes go out without a final review, causing wrong pricing and lost business.
- A dried up pipeline because key executives stopped developing new business while they focused on delivering current business.

I am sure each of you reading this have your own examples from organizations you run. Now this is your chance to correct them. Go out and find one, just one, and make it better. Once you have done that, go out, find another one, and make it better.

You know where to find these opportunities. The problem is that you try to tackle them all at once. Pick one. Find that product that can be improved and sold to help gain market share. Find that process that is so cumbersome that it makes your employees crazy. Find that group of customers that no one has contacted in a while. Do something, anything, to move one of these initiatives forward.

Once you do, you will have become an expert on how to find money where others do not normally look. The best part about becoming an expert is that you can use that expertise over and over again with future opportunities.

CHAPTER 24

Under-promising and *Not* Over-delivering

I was recently working with a large international chain of not-for-profit health and fitness centers, and one of the first things I told them was that they were giving their customers too much value. They looked at me as if I had just spoken in a foreign language they did not understand. "There is no such thing as delivering too much value to customers," a member of the senior team told me. Would you care to wager on that?

I went on to explain to them that it costs $1,500 per year for a family to join one of their facilities. That $1,500 includes access to gyms, programs, swimming lessons, and many other amenities. If I were to sign up for those same programs individually and at different places (as many families do), it would cost me more than $4,000. I explained that they were giving away more than $4,000 worth of services and only charging $1,500 for them. That is what I mean by over-delivering.

Every one of your customers has an expectation of what you will provide. What the quality will be. What the speed will be. What the price will be. Over-delivering means that you are exceeding those expectations *unnecessarily*. It means you are providing value where your customer does not expect it or where the customer does not value it.

Microsoft Excel is an example of this (as are many software programs). Most users only use about 10 percent of the features that Excel offers; so why bother building the rest of them? For the majority of users, there is no extra value for those features. Microsoft over-delivered on that product.

Conversely, many of the applications being built now are not focused on unnecessary bells and whistles that customers do not want or need. Uber is a basic app combining payment technology with GPS technology.

There is nothing fancy about it, yet it is one of the fastest-growing, most disruptive technologies the world has seen in a long time. A simple app that stores your profile information, knows where you are located, and knows where Uber drivers near you are located. Then simple matching technology to connect the customer with the driver. It delivers on exactly what customers expect.

The key to not over-delivering is to know what expectations your customers have. Once you know what they expect, you may decide to exceed them, but you will certainly know what it takes to meet those expectations.

Let us look at a few examples.

Costco is a chain of low-cost, high-volume stores with a very loyal customer base. Costco customers expect two things—low prices and a huge variety of products. People do not shop at Costco to get great service. In fact, if you have ever been to a Costco, you know there is virtually no service. There are few employees on the floor to help you, and the cash is just an assembly line of people buying things. Costco could decide to add more employees on the floor to improve service, but that would have very little value to the customer. Customers do not go to Costco for service.

At the other end of the spectrum, Four Seasons Hotels and Resorts are known for the level of service they provide. Guests at these hotels expect impeccable service and amenities. They expect to have everything they want at their fingertips. In addition, they are willing to pay a premium for it. No one goes to a Four Seasons hotel if they are looking for a good deal on a hotel room. Four Seasons employees know this and they treat every guest like a king or a queen. They could over-deliver and add a free breakfast or discounted room rate, but that is not what their customers expect. They expect a premium experience for a premium price.

Over-delivering means that you are providing additional stuff to your customer that is not of any value to them. Thus, it is costing you time, money, or reputation without adding any value to your relationship with customers. How many times have you read about a company and asked, "Why would they do that?" I ask myself that question all the time. It usually happens when I see an organization doing more than they need to in order to attract and retain customers.

How Not to Over-deliver

In order to ensure that you are not over-delivering to your customers, you need to follow these three steps:

1. Understand what the expectations of your customers are, based on a few key factors. What do customers expect in these areas?
   - Speed
   - Quality
   - Price
   - Service
   - Access
2. Determine what it will take to meet those expectations. What do we need to do to keep customers coming back?
3. Identify any additional things you can do that would be of value to your customers. What can we do that would exceed customer expectations and be of additional value to customers?

Lower-end hotels offer free Internet access (or at least include it in the room rate so that it is not an additional charge for the guest).

Car dealers include 1 year of free gas or free maintenance on the purchase of a new car.

Medical device manufacturers offer free training and upgrades on their devices.

Gyms offer free trial classes for new members.

These are all examples of organizations delivering something that exceeds the expectations of their customers and is something that customer's value. When you do that, it becomes easier to attract and retain your ideal customers.

CHAPTER 25

Operational Transparency

If you have never heard the term "operational transparency" before, then I am a happy camper because it means I coined a new phrase. Operational transparency is just as it sounds—providing transparency in the way you operate, both internally and externally. Let us deal with them separately.

External Operational Transparency

One of the best examples of external operational transparency is FEDEX and UPS. For those of you who have ever sent a package with them, you know how easy it is to track the delivery of your package. However, it was not always that way. Remember the days when you had to call customer service to find out why your package had not arrived at its destination? I bet FEDEX and UPS do too. Those types of calls used to represent the majority of calls their customer service representatives received.

They knew where the packages were and they knew by when they would arrive. So why not offer that information to the customer? By offering a website and a tracking number, not only could the customer track his or her own package, it also dramatically reduced the number of phone calls customer service representatives received. This new way of doing business was brilliant for many reasons as follows:

- It reduced the administrative (and financial burden) on FEDEX and UPS.
- It gave the customer access to real-time delivery information about their package.
- It empowered the customer to take control of the order.

Everybody wins! The customer can see the status of the package in the matter of a few seconds, and FEDEX and UPS no longer field phone calls about the status of every package. They do not waste fielding calls from customers asking, "Where is my package?" They have put that onus on the customer and made it in the customer's best interests because they provide real-time information about the location of the package.

Every inquiry a customer makes is failure work, and the more transparent you are, the less failure work you will do. Operational transparency reduces the time and effort spent on answering basic questions and inquiries. So how do you make yourself more transparent externally? Here are some questions to consider:

- What information is available to us that would be valuable to customers and/or suppliers (think package location for FEDEX customers)?
- Are we comfortable sharing that information (it needs to be accurate)?
- What types of questions do we receive most frequently from customers and business partners? Can we offer any tools that allow customers and business partners to access this information on their own?

We can boil it down to three key factors when determining whether or not to be externally transparent:

- Valuable information—delivery information, lead times, pricing (think car dealers), industry trends
- Accurate information
- Improved experience—reduces customer workload, timeline, and frustration and increases engagement and loyalty

Do you have information that would be useful for a customer or business partner to have?

Do you have accurate information to share?

Would this information improve the customer's experience? Can it reduce failure work?

If yes to all three questions, why not do something about it?

How Transparent Do You Want to Be?

When considering your next steps before implementing operational transparency, you first have to decide how transparent you want to be. In some cases, like the FEDEX example earlier, there are advantages to being fully transparent. In other cases, you might benefit more from being translucent, or even opaque.

There are four factors to consider when determining how transparent you want to be. Figure 25.1 shows those fours factors and what the different levels of transparency might look like for your organization.

1. **Information**: What information will you provide customers so that you can drive why they contact you? FEDEX benefits from being *transparent* by providing customers with complete information—a package tracking number and a website. This way, customers will not call and ask, "Where is my package?"

2. **Access**: How much access do you want to give your customers? Should it be easy or difficult for them to contact you? The Yahoo Fantasy Sports websites benefit from being *opaque*. When customers try to contact them with a question, there is no phone number, and e-mails are not returned for 24 to 36 hours. By then, customers have usually figured out a solution or moved on.

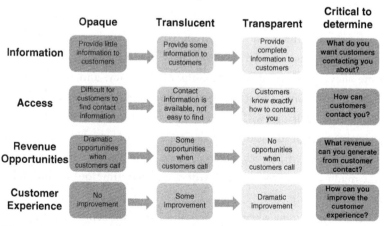

Figure 25.1 Levels of operational transparency

3. **Revenue Opportunities**: What revenue can you generate from customers contacting you? Some businesses, like cell phone providers, can generate revenue by being *opaque*. They need customers to call them so that they can offer new services and wireless packages.

4. **Customer Experience**: Can you improve the customer experience through your level of transparency? Apple provides a better customer experience by being *translucent* about new products. They leak out enough information to get customers interested, but not enough that they know everything.

You have to be thoughtful about how you look at each of these factors. Is there more of a benefit to giving the customer more information than keeping it from them? Are there more revenue opportunities if you drive customers to contact you? If you provide more information or better access, will it improve the customer experience or make no difference at all?

These are the types of questions you need to be asking when determining the right level of transparency.

Internal Operational Transparency

Have you ever had to field questions from employees about how decisions are made? Decisions about hiring, performance, growth, or strategy? If so (and you know you all have answered these questions), then you are not transparent enough in your internal operations.

How do you respond to those questions—are you transparent?

Internally, the more transparent you are, the less your employees take up time wondering about how decisions are made, the less time they spend complaining about bureaucracy, and the less time they are frustrated about the approval process. If you set parameters about how decisions will be made, whether those be investment decisions, strategic decisions, or decisions about which ideas will be implemented, employees will not waste time asking why a decision was made a certain way. They will spend less time questioning and more time doing.

Employees know when their organization is not being transparent. It discourages trust. It causes doubt to creep in about how genuine the organization and its leaders are. Moreover, once doubt creeps in, retention becomes a lot more difficult. Why would anyone want to work for an organization he or she does not trust?

Be clear and transparent about how the organization will make decisions and prioritize initiatives. Share as much relevant information as you can with employees to improve performance. The more employees know, the less they do not know. The less they do not know, the less they conjure up worst-case scenarios. The less they conjure up worst-case scenarios, the more time they spend being productive.

When employees know how decisions will be made, they will begin to self-select based on the parameters that have been communicated.

If I know that the company will only invest in new initiatives expected to make at least a 30 percent profit margin, I would not suggest ideas that will make a 10 percent margin.

If I know the company wants to become the largest volume producer of widgets, I would not suggest initiatives that are going to cut back on production volume to save money.

As I have discussed many times in this book, everything stems from having a clearly communicated ideal future state. Internal operational transparency comes from being open and transparent about how that ideal future state will be achieved.

Have you set specific performance expectations on each employee?

Do employees know how their performance is going to be measured and what steps will be taken to help them develop?

I met with a $300 million organization with more than 3,000 employees and the CEO told me that they have identified high-potential employees in their organization, but those employees have not been told they were high potentials and there was no plan in place for their development. That is not transparency. The following are what I told them to do:

- Determine the characteristics exhibited by a high-potential employee.
- Identify who the high-potential employees are.
- Tell them that they have been identified as a high-potential employee.
- Communicate their options for development.
- Monitor them to ensure they are continuously being challenged.

They were transparent about what they expected from their employees and gave them the opportunity to thrive.

Remember the three key factors to operational transparency and then you can apply them either internally or externally:

- Useful information
- Accurate information
- Information that improves the customer/employee experience and/or reduces your organization's failure work

CHAPTER 26

Leveraging Technology to Achieve Your One Priority

Everyone loves technology. Technology is cool. It is exciting. It is fast moving. However, it can also drain resources and time from your organization at an alarming pace.

I spent many years managing large technology implementations for big companies, and the themes were almost always the same. Too much time was spent on the technology side of things, and not enough time was spent on the business side. After 12 to 18 months, companies would be no better off, despite having spent hundreds of thousands of dollars (or much more) on a fancy new system.

When you take it down to the simplest common denominator, technology is about data. In order to best leverage technology to reduce costs and help accelerate growth, you need to effectively use the information that you are being provided with.

When you implement a new purchasing system, not only should basic processes be automated (purchase order generation, invoicing, and so on), but there should also be access to information that you did not have before (spend information, supplier information, pricing information, and user information), and it should be in an easy-to-use format.

When you implement a customer relationship management system (CRM), not only should all of your contact and customer information be stored, but you should also have the ability to see trends in the customer relationship (how many meetings on an average it takes to close a sale, who are sales representatives meeting with, whether length of time correlates to deal size, and so on).

When you implement a new Enterprise Resource Planning (ERP) system, not only should all of the back-end processes be automated, but you should also have faster access to better information about your company.

If you do not improve the information that you have and use it more effectively to help your organization, why bother implementing new technology? It all comes down to two simple questions as follows:

- What information do we need to help accelerate the growth of our business?
- How can we use technology to get it?

You should never start with the technology question first. Organizations that start by choosing the technology end up getting bogged down with too much information and throw money at the technology to try and make it useful. Sound familiar? Always start with the business need and the outcome you are trying to achieve.

Take this little test to see how effectively you are using technology.

1. Do we know what information will help us accelerate growth?
2. Do we capture that information now?
3. Do we use that information effectively to accelerate growth?
4. Do we share and apply that information across the organization?
5. Do we know the expected outcome of using that information effectively?

How many of those questions did you respond "Yes" to? Maybe two or three? Maybe four? If you answered "Yes" to all five, congratulations. You are effectively using information and data to grow your business. If you answered "No" to any of those questions, you need to go back to what I said earlier. . .

Effective use of technology starts with understanding the ideal outcome from using the technology and how it ties back to accelerating the growth of your business.

The use of technology should tie back to the one priority you identified earlier in the book.

I was recently speaking with an executive at a financial management company. Their one priority was to create more loyalty with their customers while reducing their administrative burden (they wanted to be more operationally transparent—see Chapter 25). This company started out by printing checks for banks customers. Customers would log onto a website, order their checks, and they would be delivered within a few days. The most frequent question this company received was, "Where are my checks?"

They focused on their one priority—creating more loyalty with customers and reducing their administrative burden—and then asked, "How can technology help us?" They decided to provide customers access to the online tracking system so that they could see when the checks would be delivered. Similar to the FEDEX and UPS example in Chapter 25, by using technology, this company was able to give customers the access they needed to check the status of their order.

This initiative saved the company more than $500,000 per year, allowed the customer service representatives to focus on customer issues where they could add value, and created more loyalty with the customers because they were more engaged in the process. This financial management company could not have done this 20 years ago, because the technology to do so did not exist. They had a clear business outcome in mind and found an effective way to use technology to help achieve it. Another benefit of this was that their customer base grew. They no longer needed to add more customer service representatives to deal with the volume.

Technology is much more scalable than human beings. It takes a lot less effort to cover a lot more ground.

There are lots of shiny new apps and technologies out there. They all claim that they can help your organization grow, increase profitability, improve customer engagement, reduce costs, increase employee retention, and drive innovation—the key is figuring out what is right for you. It means figuring out what data would be most useful to you. Go back to your one priority from Chapter 14 and then ask yourself, "How can technology help us achieve that one priority faster and more effectively?" Once you know what you want, it becomes much easier to find and exploit.

CHAPTER 27

Onboarding New Customers More Quickly

I want you to take a few minutes to think about the steps required for you to bring on a new customer. These are the steps you must go through once you have already acquired a new customer. Go ahead, here is some space to do it (try to list the steps in order).

1.
2.
3.
4.
5.
6.
7.
8.
9.
10.

Many of you probably listed things like, "Enter new customer information into CRM database," or "Create new customer profile," or "Send customer onboarding documents."

The reason I asked you to take some time out and think about this process is that most organizations I speak with have never taken the time out to look at how they onboard new customers. Not only can it be an area for improvement, it can also be cultivated as a competitive advantage. Your customer onboarding process can actually help you acquire more customers. Let me explain.

A medical product manufacturer client of mine was having trouble converting new customers from the products of their previous suppliers. It was taking too long for customers to start actually buying my client's products. This was causing numerous challenges for my client, namely that they were not recognizing revenue quickly enough from the use of their products, and that over the course of a 3- to 5-year contract, they were not able to deliver the promised savings to the customer. In some cases, it was taking customers almost a year to transition over to my client's products.

We looked at some of the key challenges customers face when they need to convert from one product manufacturer to another. We identified areas like marketing the new products to the end users so that they knew a change was coming, using up all of the old products before re-stocking inventory with the new ones, and a complete lack of resources on the customer's end to update databases and procurement systems with the new product information. I then asked my client, "Can you help customers do any of these things?" Of course, the response was, "Absolutely!"

Therefore, we went on to build a customer onboarding process that gave new customers a clear road map on what steps needed to be taken in order to convert to the new products. My client also offered support in those key areas, taking pressure off the customers' resources. The expected result was immediate. Conversion time was reduced by more than 15 percent almost immediately. That meant customers were using my client's products much sooner, and the revenue was being generated faster.

We then leveraged this onboarding process to help my client acquire new customers. This onboarding process became a competitive advantage for them. They were the first in the industry to share the process openly with both customers and potential customers. The potential customers appreciated the transparency and gaining a better understanding of what was involved in converting from one set of products to another. Customers began choosing my client because they gained a reputation for making the transition easy for the customer.

That is how you use customer onboarding to accelerate growth.

Go back to the steps that you listed earlier in this chapter and consider the following questions:

- What are we asking the customer to do that we could support them on or even do for them?
- What are the barriers that would stop customers from using our products or services immediately? What can we do to remove or lessen those barriers?
- What information do we have or use, that if shared with the customer, would improve our reputation?
- What are we asking the customer to do that is not required?
- What are we doing that is not required?
- What are other ways some of these steps can be completed?

Using the aforementioned questions against your current customer onboarding process, you should be able to identify some areas of improvement. What are they?

1.
2.
3.

The key to accelerating growth through the customer onboarding process is to find something that is of value to your customer. Too often, the onboarding process focuses on what the selling organization needs (customer information, access to people and inventory locations, product databases, and so on). Consider how you can use the onboarding process to make things easier for your customer.

When you make things easier for your customer, you thereby create more loyalty, improve your reputation, and more customers want to buy from you.

How can you change your customer onboarding process to make things easier for your customer while accelerating and improving results for you?

PROFITABILITY CATEGORY #8
Your Crystal Ball

CHAPTER 28

Shining Up Your Crystal Ball

Unfortunately, none of us has a crystal ball that we can look into and see the future. If we did, we would not make mistakes. The most successful companies, however, do their best to use discipline, common sense, and critical thinking to best exploit opportunities. By becoming better at identifying and exploiting opportunities, you will become a more successful organization.

This chapter focuses on how to better assess and exploit new opportunities. Too many organizations pursue every opportunity that comes their way and it hurts their ability to grow quickly and successfully. This chapter gives you strategies on how to identify those opportunities that can have the biggest impact. Usually, becoming better at assessing and pursuing new opportunities means you actually pursue fewer opportunities.

I had this conversation early on with a new client a few months ago. He brought me in to help his organization win more business through competitive procurement processes. The first thing I told him was, "The way you are going to win more business is by participating in fewer opportunities." I thought he was going to throw me out of his office. Sales organizations like to pursue every opportunity. I went on to explain that one has a better chance of closing business when you pursue those opportunities that align with your strengths, competitive advantages, relationships, ideal customers, and strategic direction.

The following assessment is one that I have used successfully with clients across North America and it has helped every single one of those clients accelerate growth and dramatically increase revenues. It provides them the discipline to assess every opportunity with the same decision-making criteria, with a focus on growth potential, relationship, and alignment with corporate direction.

Think of an opportunity you are considering pursuing and score yourself on each of the 10 statements in Figure 28.1.

Give each statement a score from 1 to 4 based on the scoring legend.

Additional questions to consider:

- What additional insights do we have about the customer organization?
- Was price a significant component of the evaluation criteria? If yes, can we compete on price?

	Statement	Scoring 4 = Strongly agree 3 = Moderately agree 2 = Moderately disagree 1 = Strongly disagree
1	We knew about the opportunity before it was made public or open to other competition.	
2	We had involvement/influence in the decision-making criteria the customer will use.	
3	The prospective customer's needs fit well with the solutions we offer.	
4	This is a current or past customer, or a customer of another division of our company.	
5	We have a good relationship with key influencers in the prospective customer's organization.	
6	There is a low level of competition for the prospective customer's business.	
7	There is high future growth potential with the prospective customer.	
8	The level of effort required to acquire the customer is justified by the possible results that can be achieved.	
9	There is a low amount of effort required to bring them on as a new customer (or retain them as an existing customer).	
10	There are other solutions we can offer that would be of value to the prospective customer.	
	Total Score	

Figure 28.1 Opportunity assessment matrix

Now do the same thing with an opportunity that you recently pursued and was successful. What was your score?

Now do it again with an opportunity that you recently pursued and was not successful. What was your score?

Do you see any Pattern?

Usually, when I implement this assessment with clients, we customize the statements to better fit their business. We then go back 12 to 18 months and retroactively assess past opportunities against this customized assessment. We always see a trend. **The opportunities that scored higher tended to be the most successful, and the ones that scored lower were not successful.** In some cases, we were even able to develop a threshold where the client knew to stop pursuing any opportunity below a certain score.

This is how you improve your ability to assess and exploit opportunities—by pursuing the best opportunities.

Use this assessment. Develop one of your own. Change the statements to fit your own business. The key is instilling discipline in decision making so that you pursue the best opportunities and can maximize their impact.

Do you pursue only the best opportunities or every opportunity that comes your way?

Final Thoughts

Pursuing Excellence, Not Perfection

I was meeting with a prospective client recently and said those four key words to her, "In order to achieve your objectives, we need to *pursue excellence not perfection*." After I said it, she looked at me, stood up, and said, "Can you please excuse me for a minute?" I was not sure what just happened, but I knew it was profound. Two minutes later, she returned with the CEO and the three of us proceeded to have an engaging 90-minute discussion on how we could improve the performance of their people and their organization.

When we pursue excellence, we reward improvement. We provide a clear road map for people to follow. We achieve incremental successes. In addition, we are always able to redefine what excellence means and set new expectations.

When we pursue perfection, we do not reward improvement. We only reward perfection. What if it is never achieved? There are only two possible outcomes when you strive for perfection: success and failure. There is no middle ground. Unfortunately, most organizations that strive for perfection, fail. And even though improvements have been made, they are not celebrated, because perfection was not achieved.

The next time that same organization sets expectations, people are wary and gun shy because they remember the last time the organization failed. I had a client who told me that her Board of Directors still reviews a specific failed project at every meeting. The problem is that the project failed 5 years ago!!! And they are still dwelling on it. Why would anyone want to propose any new project if that is the way failure is treated?

In this book, I provided you 25 (or more) ways for you to accelerate growth, boost profits, and enhance performance, all without making any additional financial investments. In order to implement any of these strategies successfully, you need to change your mindset to one of pursuing excellence, not perfection. You need to celebrate each achievement and even failure. You need to encourage progress and not stagnation. Once you do that, you will see your results improve.

So I leave you with this one last question: Are you pursuing excellence and setting your organization up for success, or pursuing perfection and setting it up for failure?

Index

OTHER TITLES IN OUR SUPPLY AND OPERATIONS MANAGEMENT COLLECTION

Johnny Rungtusanatham, The Ohio State University
and Joy M. Field, Boston College, *Editors*

- *Better Business Decisions Using Cost Modeling, Second Edition* by Victor Sower and Christopher Sower
- *Improving Business Performance with Lean, Second Edition* by James R. Bradley
- *Lean Communication: Applications for Continuous Process Improvement* by Sam Yankelevitch and Claire F. Kuhl
- *An Introduction to Lean Work Design: Fundamentals of Lean Operations, Volume I* by Lawrence D. Fredendall and Matthieas Thurer
- *An Introduction to Lean Work Design: Standard Practices and Tools of Lean, Volume II* by Lawrence D. Fredendall and Matthias Thurer
- *Leading and Managing Lean* by Gene Fliedner
- *Managing and Improving Quality: Integrating Quality, Statistical Methods and Process Control* by Amar Sahay
- *Mapping Workflows and Managing Knowledge: Using Formal and Tacit Knowledge to Improve Organizational Performance, Volume I* by John Kmetz
- *Mapping Workflows and Managing Knowledge: Dynamic Modeling of Formal and Tacit Knowledge to Improve Organizational Performance, Volume II* by John Kmetz

Announcing the Business Expert Press Digital Library

Concise e-books business students need for classroom and research

This book can also be purchased in an e-book collection by your library as

- a one-time purchase,
- that is owned forever,
- allows for simultaneous readers,
- has no restrictions on printing, and
- can be downloaded as PDFs from within the library community.

Our digital library collections are a great solution to beat the rising cost of textbooks. E-books can be loaded into their course management systems or onto students' e-book readers.
The **Business Expert Press** digital libraries are very affordable, with no obligation to buy in future years. For more information, please visit **www.businessexpertpress.com/librarians**. To set up a trial in the United States, please email **sales@businessexpertpress.com**.